Toasting Temecula Wines

For GARRY —

In vino veritas!

Dick

Toasting Temecula Wines

An Illustrated Guide to California's
Temecula Wine Country
and
Surrounding Regions

By
Vick Knight, Jr.

Aristan Press
31566 Railroad Canyon Road #612
Canyon Lake, CA 92587

Revised Edition
Copyright © 1999 by Vick Knight, Jr.

Cover Design by Linda Germar Hoffman

Library of Congress Catalog Card Number 99-073165
ISBN 0-931407-06-0

Printed in the United States of America

For my Father
who taught me to appreciate the
romance of viticulture and enology

Introduction

In 1990 I received a telephone call from Loretta Scott, foods editor of *The Press-Enterprise* in Riverside County, California, asking if I would be interested in writing a column featuring the Temecula Wine Country. I had previously enjoyed some success as an amateur winemaker at numerous California competitions and had announced my retirement from such judgings earlier in the year. I readily accepted the new assignment. Having worked closely with several of the professional winemakers at the time, and competed against others during their amateur days, I felt that the rapport we had developed over the years would prove beneficial as I chronicled their successes and growth.

The intervening period has been most pleasant and rewarding as I increased my store of knowledge and learned to respect even more the intricacies of producing an outstanding vintage of varietal wines.

To single out those who have been especially helpful to me in my education would be to risk inadvertently leaving out those whose patience and counsel have been truly appreciated. Knowing this in advance, I nevertheless would like to express my special gratitude to Beverley Stureman, John Moramarco and Dwayne Helmuth of Callaway

Vineyard and Winery, Vincenzo and Audrey Cilurzo, Peter Poole of Mount Palomar, Joe Travis Hart, Phil and Carol Baily, Barrett Bird of Santa Margarita Winery, Marshall Stuart, Gerry Wilson, Maurice Car'rie and G. Budd Van Roekel, Jon McPherson of Thornton Winery, Nancy Johnston of the Temecula Valley Vintners Association, the Temecula Valley Chamber of Commerce and the Temecula Valley Wine Society.

Without their help and cooperation, the First Edition published three years ago, or this revised volume would never have been written or published.

As this was the first book dealing with the wine industry in the Temecula Valley, it was important to have the facts correct, and I relied on the various winery staffs to help me compile accurate and updated information. For their assistance, I am most thankful. Any errors of commission or omission, therefore, are solely the author's.

My interest in the fruit of the vines and the making of wine dates back to my father, the late Vick Knight, Sr. He started making a few bottles of Concord wine from vines that grew in his backyard in Hollywood, California, in order to provide a modest amount of sacramental wine for the use of his son-in-law, the Reverend Robert Kelly. I learned some of the fundamentals of amateur winemaking from him and subsequently inherited his library dealing with enology and viticulture as well as much of the paraphernalia associated with the hobby. I later purchased a home in Riverside County and planted a number of varietal vines of my own, then began entering competitions with other Southern California amateurs. After winning the "Best of Show" award at the California State Fair in 1989, I retired from competition while I was ahead, and have limited my winemaking and increased my wine-writing in recent years. Judging various competitions, assisting restaurants with the development of wine lists and hosting wine-related events all are proving to be enjoyable ventures.

The fact that the Temecula Wine Country has achieved its rightful role as one of California's premier viticultural regions is well documented. Winemakers here have proven that they are more than capable of producing many of the top California varieties; this is evidenced by the number of awards garnered in competitions with wineries in other parts of the state.

What has taken place in recent years, however, is the desire and willingness of local winemakers to experiment with varietals not previously known to thrive in the unique microclimate present in Temecula. Many grapes indigenous to the Southern Rhone Valley and Italy thrive in Temecula, and these wines have captured an untapped share of the consumer market. This is the direct result of a cadre of professionally trained winemakers who have dared to experiment and winery owners who have supported their efforts. The Temecula Valley Vintners Association is a networking and mutual benefit organization dedicated to advancing the products and reputation of Temecula wineries. Special events are sponsored annually by the Association, and participation in these activities serves to benefit individual wineries and enhance the influence of the group as a whole. The annual Temecula Balloon & Wine Festival, dinners with winemakers, Barrel and Nouveau Tastings and other events bring crowds of wine lovers and novices alike to the valley to sample products currently in release.

Another organization dedicated to the education and appreciation of wine and to providing assistance to local vintners and wineries is the Temecula Valley Wine Society, founded in 1983 by a group of local wine *aficionados*. Members meet once a month for dinner featuring either a varietal wine or a vintner and his or her wines. Food is chosen to complement the featured wine, and a speaker is asked to discuss the characteristics of a particular variety being tasted. The membership also assists with the Riverside International Wine Competition held annually at the University of California Riverside.

A scholarship fund has been established by the Society for a student in the fields of Enology, Viticulture or Wine Marketing. A splendid wine li-

> *Come, come; good wine is a good, familiar creature if it be well used; exclaim no more against it.*
> -- William Shakespeare

brary collection has been donated to the Temecula Public Library by the Society in its efforts to provide an educational focus to its mission.

Additional information regarding the activities of the Temecula Valley Wine Society and its requirements for membership may be obtained by writing the Society at 41275 Cruz Way, Temecula CA 92591.

And, of course, a very special note of appreciation must go to *The Press-Enterprise* and the editor of my "Temecula Wine Country" column, Orlando Ramirez. Permission to utilize material that originally appeared in this publication over the years is what made this revised volume a reality. I am obliged for this consent and am pleased to acknowledge my sincere thanks.

Finally, as in previous books of mine, my dear and talented wife, Carolyn, somehow managed to continue to steer me through the rocks and shoals of desktop publishing in spite of my life-long resistance to all things electronic.

Vick Knight, Jr.
Canyon Lake, California
September 1999

NOTE: The phone numbers for Temecula area wineries, restaurants and hotels listed in this book do not contain area codes since the current designation, 909, will change to 951 in February of 2000.

Foreword

Why Temecula?

Over 200 years ago, winemaking made its debut in Southern California. The tradition still exists today in Temecula. Over the last 30 years, the grapevines have matured with the loving care of the Temecula valley grape growers, and their vines are second to none.

Being situated 22 miles from the Pacific Ocean, 1500 feet above sea level, the Temecula valley's rolling vineyards are the best place to grow premium quality wine grapes that allow the winemakers to create world class wines.

As I travel internationally tasting wines and visiting vineyards, I am convinced now more than ever that the Temecula valley is the best place in the world to grow premium quality wine grapes. I invite you to visit our wineries and taste the quality of the valley for yourself. I would enjoy hearing your opinion.

Enjoy this book dedicated to the Temecula Valley Wine Country. It will provide you with a first hand view if this new and exciting wine region. Enjoy!

John A. Moramarco
Senior Vice-President
General Manager
Callaway Vineyard & Winery

Table of Contents

Mission San Gabriel in Los Angeles County was the site of California's first winery.

In the Beginning

While no diary still in existence provides an exact date, it's believed that Father Junipero Serra is responsible for bringing the first Vinifera grapevine cuttings from Baja California and planting them at Mission San Diego in 1769, although some accounts place the event as taking place at Mission San Juan Capistrano several years later. Since it takes a few years for cuttings to bear enough fruit to successfully make juice for fermentation, it appears that California's wines may well date back to the nation's Independence in 1776. The planting of grapevines was such a common occurrence in those days that it lacked the importance of being properly documented in the journals of the time.

Franciscan Friars, then, must be given recognition as California's initial winemakers. They held that role exclusively for more than half a century, producing vintages for Father Serra's chain of twenty-one missions up and down El Camino Real to be utilized for sacramental, medicinal and table purposes. These grapes were what we term the Mission variety, still utilized today, principally in the production of dessert wines, ports and sherries. These blue-black Mission grapes are thought to be a variety of Spain's Monica grape, probably brought to the New World by early conquistadors.

1

Almost all of these Franciscan Missions had vineyards and adjacent wineries. While the padres were advised by their superiors to limit their distribution and trade only with others in their order, it wasn't long before sales of wine and brandy to neighboring rancheros and itinerant traders began to materialize. Governor Diego Borica of California issued directives designed to restrict this trade and discourage the practice, but his decrees were generally ignored. However, when it was brought to his attention that export of California wines could become advantageous to the young region's economy, he withdrew his instructions and advocated that vineyard acreage be expanded for commercial purposes.

Father Junipero Serra planted the first wine grapes at Mission San Diego.

Two missions located in what is now Los Angeles County were among the major California wine producers of the period; they were the San Fernando and San Gabriel Missions. To this day, visitors to San Gabriel Mission can observe the remains of the winery operation, said to once make an annual yield of four hundred barrels of wine and two hundred barrels of brandy.

It wasn't until secularization of the Franciscan missions in 1830 that the first commercial vineyards began to appear in and around Los Angeles. The padres had developed a profitable sideline of making and selling brandy from their grapes to the area's pioneer residents of both American and Spanish heritage, and this fact didn't escape certain of their customers.

It was soon obvious that Southern California's soil and climate were especially conducive to the production of grapes. Joseph Chapman is generally credited as being California's first American vintner. He learned the basics of grape growing and winemaking from the mission padres and then went about planting four thousand vines between 1824 and 1826 in Los Angeles. His success led to additional plantings by other immigrants such as Louis Bouchet, William Logan, William George Chard and Andrew Boyle.

But it took the knowledge and efforts of a professional viticulturist from the Bordeaux region in France to import European varieties in 1833 and plant the cuttings in 104 acres of land he had acquired west of the Los Angeles River. Thus Jean Louis Vignes is celebrated as the father of California's wine industry. It was Don Louis del Aliso, as Vignes was to be known, who was responsible for importing selective and choice grapevines from European sources. His success and reputation in utilizing French winemaking traditions soon encouraged others to follow his lead and plant extensive vineyards. Aliso and Vignes

Streets in what was once El Pueblo de la Riena de los Angeles were a part of his El Aliso Vineyard, acreage that in later times was utilized in the construction of the Los Angeles Union Station Railroad Terminal. Some claim that Vignes also planted vines in the Temecula Valley but later abandoned this venture.

Southern California's vineyards began to grow, with the success of Vignes' initial vintage in 1837 in Los Angeles. Many well-known contemporary locations in Southern California once were vineyards. These include Boyle Heights, the site of Andrew Boyle's vines; Santa Anita Racetrack, one-time location of "Lucky" Baldwin's twelve hundred-acre holdings; and Anaheim's Disneyland, the location in the 1870s of one of the principal California wine districts. Unfortunately, Anaheim's vineyards were wiped out in 1884 by a virus known as Pierce's Disease.

By the early Twentieth Century, the Cucamonga Valley became the leading area producing wine grapes in Southern California. From the foothills of the Sierra Madre Mountains in Etiwanda to Alta Loma, Ontario, Guasti and the northwestern boundaries of Riverside County, vineyards flourished until the eventual advent of real estate developers and commercial inroads.

What Tiburcio Tapia had initially planted on lands obtained in 1839 by a land grant from the Mexican government had grown to a famed wine-growing district. By 1920 and the approach of Prohibition, San Bernardino County was estimated to have a vineyard of twenty thousand acres, one of the largest in the world. This was at a time when the plantings in Napa County and Sonoma were just beginning to increase. The Volstead Act put an end to the commercial production and sale of most spirits in the United States, and the Guasti Winery made the best of the situation facing it. This was accomplished by modifying production to lawful kosher and sacramental wines and the transporting of fresh grapes to home winemakers who became known as "bootleggers." Grape concentrate also was produced at the time by numerous California wineries unable to legally make wine. This was marketed with the warning that the addition of yeast was not advised as this would cause the juice to ferment.

It's easy to surmise that not many who purchased the grape concentrate observed this admonition.

Following Repeal of Prohibition in 1933, the Cucamonga region continued to grow until World War II. At that time the boom in industrial and housing needs occurred, bringing urban sprawl and increased air-befouling smog. A massive steel plant and the Ontario International Airport, as well as factories and residential tracts, took over what once were verdant vineyards. In addition, the cost of acreage made it difficult for vintners to economically maintain their properties, even with the tax advantages of agricultural preserve status.

From one of the descendants of the Brookside Vineyard Company, founded in 1832 and one of the oldest in the state, emerged the new wine district of the Temecula Valley. The late Philo Biane began his quest in 1959 to discover new locations to grow premium varietal grapes. Marius Biane, Philo's grandfather, emigrated from France's southwestern region of Gascony in 1892 and became winemaker for the pioneer Vaché family and later purchased his own vineyards in 1916. Biane continued in his family's business and in 1952 managed to re-establish the Brookside Vineyard Company at Ontario. He later acquired the venerable Guasti Winery and began to utilize its underground cellars for aging purposes.

Philo Biane discovered that the Temecula region was free from smog, had the requisite soil to support varietal grape production and was rela-

> *Take a little wine for thy stomach's sake.*
> *-- I Timothy 5:23*

5

The Italian Swiss Colony in Asti operated one of the world's major wineries at the turn of the century. tively secure at the time from urbanization. In 1965, the Kaiser-Aetna Development Company planned a community of residences, ranches and commercial centers and held some seven hundred acres in reserve for agricultural purposes, chiefly fruit trees and vineyards. Biane saw the obvious advantages of this mesa with its unique microclimate. It was warm during the day and cooled at night through easterly ocean breezes directed through the "Rainbow Gap" in the Santa Margarita Pass of the nearby Coastal Mountain Range. The area was just twenty-two miles from the Pacific Ocean. It was believed that these valleys and rolling hills would provide an envronment similar to the premium wine-producing regions of Northern California and Europe. In cooperation with local agricultural officials and experts from the University of California's Davis Enological School, Biane learned that wells could supply ample water to irrigate this arid range land. Thus he established his initial sprinkler and drip-irrigated vineyards.

Kaiser-Aetna employed a farm advisor named Dick Break to assist those considering developing vineyards in the region. He was a graduate of UC Davis and had extensive experience in the Coastal Valley with the consulting firm of Miles and Cullington.

It wasn't long before these professional viticulturalists began sharing their knowledge and expertise with others, and Vincenzo Cilurzo, Ely Callaway, Leon Borel, Ben Drake and John Poole were among the first to be convinced that the Temecula Valley would be an ideal place for them to establish vineyards for themselves and grow premium varietal grapes.

Were it not for these pioneers and their vision, coupled with an enthusiasm for the best in viticultural conditions, the Temecula Valley might have taken another direction in its dynamic growth.

It took the Cilurzos, Callaways and Pooles, along with their subsequent associates in the Temecula Valley Vintners Association, to bring to fruition this dream. Today, more than 3,000 acres of premium varietal grape vines are to be found in the verdant Temecula Valley. A chronology of the numerous accomplishments, recognition and growth of those who set the stage will follow.

In 1984, the Bureau of Alcohol, Tobacco and Firearms officially recognized the Temecula Appellation as a premium varietal grape-growing region, more than two centuries after the Franciscan missionaries planted their first vineyards.

Vincenzo Cilurzo is surrounded here by a few of his favorite things.

Cilurzo Vineyard & Winery

Some ten thousand miles separate Southern Italy's Calabria region from Southern California's Riverside County, but there are some parallels that quickly reveal themselves to those who like to make comparisons. Each boasts a Mediterranean climate with hot, dry summers, and bright sunny weather prevails throughout most of the year. Fruits and vegetables are grown in abundance, with grapes among the major crops. Giuseppe Cilurzo left Calabria in 1913 to come to America, bringing with him a family tradition for winemaking.

Fifty-four years later, in 1967, his son, Vincenzo, purchased a hundred-acre parcel in the Temecula Valley. On the advice of consultant Dick Break from UC Davis, he planted that district's first vineyard of premium varietal grapes the following year, and began to make plans for a small winery and the eventual construction of a home built of adobe bricks.

Vincenzo ("Vince" to his many friends and associates) Cilurzo was an ABC-TV Emmy Award-winning lighting director. He and his wife, Audrey, lived at the time in Hollywood's Los Feliz neighborhood in a large home once occupied by the legendary cowboy actor Tom Mix. It was a two-story structure with stained glass windows and numerous custom features. Vince's original thought was to look into the possibility of transporting that house the ninety miles south to the property he'd bought in Temecula, but the logistics of that move convinced him that it was impractical.

Then came the dream of an adobe hacienda.

When the director first moved from New York to California in 1950, he learned of the properties and style of structures fashioned from adobe and acquired a single hand-made adobe brick. As the years went by, he visited numerous adobe homes, and one in Flintridge especially intrigued him. It was afterwards that the Cilurzos began to seriously make their future plans.

Quickly, bring me

a beaker of wine.

--Aristophanes

"I heard of a builder in San Diego County, Jack Weir, who had the reputation of being the Frank Lloyd Wright of adobe construction," he says today. "With Weir, Audrey and I set out to design our dream house and made frequent trips to Mexico where we sought out native artisans from whom we bought wrought iron lighting and fireplace fixtures."

The couple and their youngsters moved from Hollywood to their burgeoning vineyard in 1978 and lived in a mobile home on the site as construction began. Their new single-level home was to contain 3,480 square feet of living space plus a three-car garage. The hand-made adobe bricks came from a plant in Fresno and were fabricated from a combination of sand, silt and adobe soil, sun-dried in the traditional manner. Each weighed forty-eight pounds, was eighteen inches wide, twelve inches in length and four inches high. The entire structure was reinforced to meet code standards and provide earthquake protection.

Massive used wooden beams from San Diego's old Point Loma High School were sand-blasted and termite-proofed and became the overhead supports. Similar recycled building materials were used for cabinets. Mexican floor and roof tiles completed the desired ambiance of the Cilurzo residence. The original adobe brick that Vincenzo had acquired a quarter of a century earlier is incorporated into the wall adjacent to the home's ornate Mexican crafted wooden entry doors. The brick had earlier suffered the ignominy of being run over by a delivery truck during the construction phase, but enough of it survived to become a part of the completed structure. While comparable adobe fabrication today is in the range of $200 per square foot, 1978 costs were appreciably less and this, coupled with the family's penchant for prudent shopping in nearby Mexico, held expenditures to a minimum.

Ceramic tiles bearing a grape motif dominate the kitchen, capping a free-standing range island and covering the sink and counters. Vaulted adobe arches provide visual contact between interior spaces, and terra cotta pipes are inset into walls to store and display Vince and Audrey's impressive personal wine collection.

The environmentally conscious Cilurzos designed an energy efficient water-to-air heat pump

Known as the "Tre Paisani," the team of winemakers at Cilurzo are, left to right, Don Frangipani, Vince Cilurzo and Dr. Enrique Ferro.

11

CILURZO

Since 1968

APRIL and LUISĒNO VINEYARDS
MERLOT
Temecula
1997

B.W. 4867 ALCOHOL 13.5% BY VOLUME

*Cilurzo's Reserve 1997
Merlot won many awards.*

to air condition and warm their home. Solar panels, ideal in the sunny microclimate of the Temecula Valley, heat a fifteen-by-thirty foot swimming pool, the focal point of a patio just outside the home. A pump converts heat from the pool to energy which, in turn, operates the air conditioner. In the winter, the action is reversed, taking full advantage of the superb insulating benefits of the adobe construction.

"It's a reversal of the concept by which refrigerators operate," Vincenzo explains, "and it also serves to keep our hot tub at a comfortable temperature. Our home is all-electric, and a second set of solar panels provides for the family's hot water needs."

The homesite is located on a three-acre plateau overlooking the family vineyard and winery and includes an orchard of assorted fruit trees along with a three-quarter acre pond stocked with catfish. Peacocks, ducks, a blue heron and various migratory species can be seen from a small shaded picnic area surrounded by tables, benches and parking spaces.

Situated a scant hundred yards west of the house, the Cilurzo Winery occupies a 13,500 square foot structure with half of the operation at underground level. Tours and a tasting room are features for many visitors to the Temecula Valley Wine Country, but the Cilurzos boast of being the first of the dozen or so members of the Temecula Valley Vintners Association to actually live on the property where their grapes are grown and wines produced.

Cilurzo and his team of winemakers preside over the day-to-day operations of the winery producing more than twelve thousand cases of red and white wines annually, with plans to expand to twenty- five thousand cases. About twenty-five percent of the grapes grown come from their own vineyards, the rest from other Temecula parcels. Innovative practices at the winery have resulted in three different versions of the estate-grown Petite Sirah grapes. Their nouveau was initially introduced in 1987 and quickly became a favorite of many consumers. It's an intensely fruity wine and, unlike many nouveaus, has the lasting power to remain fresh for at least two years. Cilurzo's Petite Sirahs have been consistent medal winners at major competitions and were voted the "Best Varietal of the Temecula Region" at a recent California State Fair. A late-harvest Sirah is also available in 375-ml form in limited quantities. Each represents the Cilurzo style of full-bodied reds that have become the signature wines of this colorful family tradition.

Among the other premium wines produced for the Cilurzo label are Chardonnay, Sauvignon Blanc, Chenin Blanc, White Zinfandel, Merlot, Cabernet Sauvignon, Muscat Canelli and a pro-

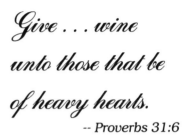

Give . . . wine unto those that be of heavy hearts.
-- *Proverbs 31:6*

13

prietary red and white blend called "Vincheno" and named after the family's children, Vinnie and Chenin.

Some forty years ago, the California Prestige Wine Society was formed to promote and gain greater appreciation for the Golden State's premium wines. As an indication of the high regard that his peers have for Vince Cilurzo, he serves as a past-president of that distinguished group and is still active in serving as an outspoken advocate for the state's wine industry and those who toil in the vineyards, tasting rooms and cellars of California's myriad wineries.

An unanticipated utilization of the family home's amenities has emerged as the Cilurzo Winery's reputation has grown over the years. Winners of numerous prestigious awards year after year, Cilurzo's varietal wines attract an increasing number of tourists to Temecula for first-hand tours. This has evolved into a series of "Dinners with the Winemaker" where Audrey Cilurzo has ample opportunity to display her culinary skills, cooking tempting meals served with estate-bottled premium Cilurzo wines to complement the elements of the specific menu choices. She's prepared meals for as many as sixty in her home with an emphasis on fresh ingredients and California cuisine. Guests gather in the adobe overlooking a 360-degree vista of the surrounding countryside and neighboring vineyards. They sit either on the patio by the pool, around the kitchen, or in the dining area at a table once owned by Mary Pickford. The Cilurzos have furnished their household in an eclectic style with items and pieces collected over the years from varied sources.

One feature not usually seen in winemakers' homes–or many other homes, for that matter–are a pair of Emmy Awards, presented to Vincenzo Cilurzo in recognition of his talents as lighting director of a Las Vegas "Stars of Jazz" television spe-

CILURZO

Since 1968

Estate Bottled

PETITE SIRAH
Temecula
1997

B.W. 4867 ALCOHOL 13.8% BY VOLUME

Petite Sirah has been a consistent prize-winner for the Cilurzos.

cial and a similar role for a Merv Griffin production at Caesar's Palace. He continues to drive to Hollywood for television and photography assignments, including the popular "Jeopardy" game show.

"Sure, it's a long freeway commute to Temecula from Hollywood," he says, "still I couldn't imagine another lifestyle after experiencing this one. Once in a while, I take a look at that original adobe brick and I appreciate all the more the fact that dreams can indeed come true!"

Temecula is a long way from Italy's "boot" and the descendant's European roots, but the family's winemaking tradition abides in the lives of Vincenzo and Audrey Cilurzo and their unique and distinctive adobe homestead.

The Cilurzo Vineyard & Winery is located at 41220 Calle Contento, just a few hundred yards south of Rancho California Road. There is a $1 charge for tasting, refunded with the purchase of any of the fine Cilurzo red or white premium varietal wines. Souvenir wine glasses can be purchased for $2.50. The winery and tasting room are open daily from 9:30 a.m. to 5 p.m., with many attractive gift items available for sale, many bearing the distinctive Cilurzo logo.

Reservations for guided tours, catered brunches, luncheons or dinners, as well as additional information regarding the winery, may be obtained by calling 676-5250.

Celebrity Brooke Shields is among the many fans of Cilurzo wines.

There's a good chance that visitors will have the opportunity to meet and chat with either Vince or Audrey Cilurzo while sampling their estate grown and bottled wines.

Meet the Winemaker

Three talented and experienced winemakers have joined to form the Cilurzo Winery's "Tre Paisani," a combination unique among Temecula Valley's wine professionals.

Vince Cilurzo, whose exploits have been chronicled elsewhere on these pages, heads the team at his eponymous winery. This veteran of the wine industry decided that his marketing and enological skills might best be complemented by the abilities and artistry of others in the field, and he now serves as the captain of a team of dedicated and gifted winemakers. Each of the trio boasts a family background dating back to Italy, and thus the name "Tre Paisani" evolved and appears on their products.

A native of Allentown, Pennsylvania, Don Frangipani serves as cellar master. Don is a graduate of Penn State University with a major in Agriculture and has many years of expeience in the fields of produce and restaurant management. He joined the Cilurzo team in July of 1996.

His specialty in earlier years had been the growing and distribution of mushrooms, so working in the moist and sunless Cilurzo wine cellars is not an unusual environment for him. His family has many Italian ties and is well known in the epicurean brokerage business.

Joining Cilurzo and Frangipani to complete the threesome is Dr. Enrique Ferro. His father left Italy in 1939 to found the Santo Tomas Winery in Baja California, and Dr. Ferro followed in the family business. His training and reputation have led to his subsequent service as consultant for numerous Texas and California wineries, and he has taught classes in both Enology and Viticulture in Italy as well as the United States.

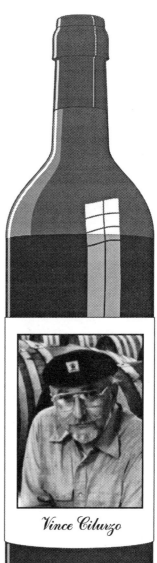

Vince Cilurzo

17

Callaway's Craig Weaver and John Moramarco inspect grape leaves to ensure quality control, using environmental methods.

18

Callaway Vineyard & Winery

In late August 1968, a real estate sales representative stopped John Moramarco along Rancho California Road, introduced his guest to John and asked him, "If you were going to establish a vineyard in this area, where would you plant it?"

John showed them the current site of Callaway Vineyard & Winery. The guest said "If I am successful in purchasing this land, would you be interested in planting it for me?" As it turned out the gentleman did purchase the land and, three months later, the two men met in Temecula and began making plans for the vineyard and winery.

The man who solicited John Moramarco's help was, of course, Ely Callaway, president of Burlington Industries of New York. He was one who thrived on taking on new and exciting business ventures and one who was seriously looking into establishing himself as a major player in the rebirth of Southern California's vineyards.

One of Callaway's first acts after completing the escrow papers was to employ John Moramarco as his viticulturist. Moramarco was an experienced grape grower with knowledge of the region's needs garnered from years with his family's vineyards and winery in the Cucamonga area.

The original planting covered 105 acres and was expanded by additional acreage five years later. In 1981, 170 acres to the west was planted as Vignes Hills Vineyard, and the four hundred-acre

Bell Vineyards were acquired in 1987, bringing Callaway's Temecula Valley vineyards to the current 750 acres.

Ely Callaway left Burlington Industries behind to concentrate his efforts on his emerging vineyard. In 1974 the original winery was constructed and the first Callaway crush became a reality. Sixteen thousand cases resulted from that vintage, a modest amount when compared to the 1995 production of one hundred, sixty-five thousand cases.

The selection of John Moramarco as viticulturist proved to be a wise decision since his experience and willingness to experiment with new techniques along with variations of tried and true procedures soon made the vineyard the envy of many others with lengthy histories in the wine industry.

Because the natural soils found in the Temecula Valley contain large amounts of decomposed granite, they are free of Phylloxera infestation, the scourge of many Northern California vineyards. This permitted Moramarco to plant grapevines on their own roots, without resorting to graftings. In this way, he was able to produce grapes with intense varietal flavors, a definite marketing advantage. In addition, Moramarco soon began training his vines in the classical technique known as the quadrilateral cordon. By assisting in the circulation of air and exposing a greater amount of the grapevine's leaves to the sun, this technique produces healthier vines and effectively fights mildew and other plant diseases.

Another technique pioneered by Callaway Vineyard and Winery was the night harvesting in 1984 of Chardonnay and Chenin Blanc varieties to guarantee that all grapes are picked at their peak ripeness. With this procedure taking place under bright artificial lights during the cooler hours of evening and early morning, crispness and full flavors are ensured.

Callaway limited its production to white wines beginning in 1982. The staff was convinced that the Temecula growing environment contained the uniform consistency needed to take advantage of the varietal character of the region. For a number of years, the winery only produced white wines.

Beverley Stureman, Dwayne Helmuth and John Moramarco are proud of Callaway's innovative techniques.

In 1976, during America's Bicentennial celebration, the Queen of England, Her Majesty Queen Elizabeth, visited the United States and was a guest at a banquet honoring America's Bicentennial anniversary at New York's Waldorf Astoria. Callaway's 1974 White Riesling was chosen to be served the Queen, following a competitive tasting of American wines. The honor of being selected to pour for the Queen was enhanced when Her Majesty, not known to be a wine drinker, requested a second glass. Knowledge of this recognition wasn't lost on others, and Callaway's white wines began to appear on retail shelves with regularity in subsequent months.

Ely Callaway, always an entrepreneur, moved on to a new challenge in 1981 and later founded Callaway Golf. His innovative "Big Bertha" clubs captured the imagination of golfers as well as their checkbooks, and yet another Callaway venture followed his success in winemaking.

Hiram Walker acquired the vineyards and winery that year and in 1987 became a component of the international food and beverage firm known as Allied Domecq, with headquarters in the United Kingdom. Allied Domecq is now responsible for the production, sales and merchandising of the wines of Callaway Vineyard & Winery as well as Atlas Peak Vineyards, Clos du Bois and the William Hill Winery.

Still another special feature of the Callaway operation is the winery's commitment to environmental sensitivity. Since 1969 Callaway has vir-

One of Callaway's popular "Rhone-style" wines is Viognier.

Callaway's Merlot has become a leading varietal favorite.

tually eliminated even spot spraying of insecticides. Natural grasses are allowed to grow between the rows of grapes to provide a home for beneficial predator insects, such as praying mantises, parasitic wasps and ladybird beetles that feed on such leaf-damaging insects as leaf-hoppers and skeletonizers. Such biological control techniques have been researched and utilized cooperatively with entomologists on the staff at the Riverside campus of the University of California. In addition, plum trees planted in the vineyard have helped to sustain helpful insects during the winter so they will be available to feed on destructive leaf hoppers when spring arrives.

In 1986 Callaway employees constructed perches in the vineyards for wild birds. As a direct result,Redtail Hawks hunt rodents during the day and owls take over the night shift to provide round-the-clock pest control.There is no need for harmful herbicides inasmuch as weeds are mechanically sliced from beneath the vines.

Perhaps the most important factor in Callaway's environmental conscienceness is through the use of water-conserving drip irrigation, a practice that saves enough water annually to supply the needs of 480 families of four.

"It's very gratifying to see that the environmental techniques we practice have also enhanced the quality of our grapes, which ultimately enables us to make fine wines," says General Manager John Moramarco. "For example, our drip irrigation system allows us to control moisture levels very precisely. We can make sure the grapes receive the right amount of water to produce a crop with the ideal sugar/acid balance to produce the fine wines we market."

Perhaps the best-known and successful of Callaway's broad selection of wines is Chardonnay. This charming white wine is aged on its yeast lees in stainless steel tanks rather than

Bring in the bottled lightening, a clean tumbler and a corkscrew.
-- *Charles Dickens*

23

in the more traditional oak barrels. The process, known as "sur-lees," produces the fresh and distinctive flavors of the grape, and the resulting wines have increased the reputation of the winery through their popularity and success across the country.

A wine unique to Callaway is "Sweet Nancy," a late-harvest Chenin Blanc that has been blessed with the "Noble Rot" of wine lore, the mold known scientifically as *Botrytis cinerea.* During those rare climatic conditions that permit this condition to occur, a dessert wine of rare and deliciously concentrated flavors is produced with fresh floral aromas and a taste reminiscent of ripe pears and guava. Produced in limited quantities in 375-milliliter bottles, the finish of this exceptional wine is both long and luscious. Other favorites at the Callaway tasting room include a Cabernet Sauvignon, Merlot, Nebbiolo Bello, Sauvignon Blanc, Chenin Blanc, and Muscat Canelli.The Callaway Chenin Blanc, incidentally, is Number

Callaway's unique late harvest Chenin Blanc is produced in limited quantities.

One in sales of this varietal in the USA.

In recent years, the winery has released in limited quantities several vintages in a widely acclaimed "Special Collection" series. These include premium wines produced from estate-grown vines grafted to mature roots going into the granitic soil almost twenty-five feet.

"With consumer interest running high for Rhone-style wines, we thought the timing of these wines was just right," says Winemaker Dwayne Helmuth. "The initial release of Viognier sold out almost overnight, and now we've added a Pinot Gris and a Dolcetto to this exclusive line."

Callaway's pemium wines have garnered more than one hundred awards, medals and ribbons in national and international competitions in recent years.

Tasting Callaway's line of fine varietal wines is an experience not to be missed. The Winery and Tasting Room are open from 10:30 a.m. to 5 p.m. daily, except for Easter Sunday, Thanksgiving, Christmas and New Year's Day.

Tours take place Monday through Friday at 11 a.m., 1 p.m. and 3 p.m. On weekends and other holidays, tours are conducted each hour between 11 a.m. and 4 p.m. A large paved parking area is available for guests, and additonal stuctures have been added in recent years to accommodate the growth of production of Callaway's wines. An extensive gift shop and hospitality center with a wide variety of unusual souvenirs and collectibles is on hand at the Visitor Center, 32720 Rancho California Road in Temecula.

There is a modest $4 charge for tasting four wines, and this includes a glass with the distinctive Callaway logo.

The Vineyard Terrace Restaurant is located on the premises overlooking the expanse of Callaway's premium grape vines to the west.

Special events, dinners, holiday tastings and

vineyard walks are scheduled annually along with a fall Harvest Festival and Grape Stomp. For details and exact dates, call (800) 472-2377 or 676-4001.

Callaway's popular Chardonnay can be found on winery shelves throughout the nation.

About the Winemaker

Dwayne Helmuth spent his early years in his native Fresno working in his family's vineyards. A basic course in Enology taken in his freshman year at Fresno State University sparked his interest in a discipline that combined his knowledge of grapes with his fascination in science. Upon completion of his undergraduate studies and a degree in Enology, Dwayne joined the staff of Guild Winery and Distilleries in 1973. Five years later, he had been promoted to manager of one of California's largest winemaking facilities at Guild Bear Creek Winery in Lodi. A visit to Callaway Vineyard & Winery three years later served to impress him with the state-of-the-art potential for optimum working conditions, and he accepted the offer to join Callaway as assistant winemaker. In 1983, Dwayne was named winemaker at Callaway. Since his first vintage, the winery's taste style has been characterized by fresh, appealing and varietally flavored wines.

According to Dwayne Helmuth, "Much of our success has been due to the unique vineyards at Callaway. Certainly the fact that we can grow our grapes on their own vinifera roots intensifies the true varietal character of the fruit. This ultimately has a positive effect on the wines we produce from these grapes."

Dwayne and his dedicated winemaking staff have continually strived to perfect the distinctive style of the winery's Chardonnay. The Callaway process of aging the lees in stainless steel tanks results in the first wine of this type produced in California.

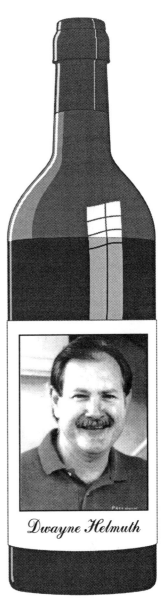

Dwayne Helmuth

John Poole founded the Mount Palomar Winery in 1969.

28

Mount Palomar Winery

Ask a Southern Californian what comes to mind when hearing the words "Mount Palomar," and the answer will probably either be "an outstanding observatory and massive telescope" or "one of the region's leading wineries." Each response would be accurate, but this would not have been the case prior to 1969. That was the year John H. Poole, a pioneer communicator with an interest in thirteen radio and television stations, sold KBIG, his Catalina Island station, and purchased and planted his eighty-acre Long Valley Vineyards in the Temecula Valley.

Poole had a checkered career before becoming a winemaker. He had worked as a tuna fisherman, merchant seaman, shipboard radio operator, U.S. Army officer, radar instructor and major player in the field of telecommunications. Married to a European-born wife, he was a world traveler and always considered wine to be a natural part of daily family meals. When he learned that a parcel of desirable land ideal for the production of premium varietal grapes was available, he lost no time in acquiring the property and arranging for irrigation and planting his first vines in Temecula. Six years later, he built the first phase of what is now the Mount Palomar Winery and produced his initial wines under that label.

John Poole's stated philosophy has been precise since the onset of his winery venture: "Produce high quality estate-bottled wines and provide

This attractive label graces Mount Palomar's award-winning "Super Tuscan" Cortese white wines.

a pleasant and educational atmosphere for visitors to the Temecula Valley Wine Country."

It's been his goal to help those visitors to the Wine Country make the understanding and enjoyment of fine wine a part of everyday life.

"I've always done my best to remove the mysticism and snobbery of wine without destroying the romantic aspects of the fermented grapes," he says. "Over the early years of the winery, I enjoyed meeting the public and conducting educational tours of the winery."

John Poole's son, Peter, now runs the winery and its corporate parent, Poole Properties, Inc. Managing the first "second generation" winery in Temecula, he has maintained the approach started by his father, while drawing on his background in plant biology and eighteen years of experience in the Temecula region to forge new and exciting directions.

Mount Palomar has expanded its tasting room and picnic facilities in increments over the years to the point that it now includes a Mediterranean-style deli featuring a wide range of fresh salads, tortas, sandwiches, pâtés, fresh bread and assorted cheeses. It's open Thursdays through Sundays. A special feature on Sundays is the Patio Grill that's offered to an appreciative crowd of visitors to the winery. With some sixty picnic tables arranged throughout the grounds in various locations, there is ample room for casual meals, all complemented with appropriate Mount Palomar wines, of course.

Those who wish to plan full lunches at the winery for private groups of twenty or more may make arrangements by calling 676-5047. The tasting room is open from 10 a.m. to 5 p.m. daily. Tasting is $3 per person, and includes a Mount Palomar logo glass and six tastes of the visitor's choice. Specialty wines may also be sampled at an additional charge.

The original vineyard of eighty acres has ex-

Vineyard Manager Vidal Perez, Peter Poole and Winemaker Etienne Cowper share a glass or two of Mount Palomar's Sangiovese.

panded to ninety-two acres, and ninety-five per-cent of Mount Palomar wines come from the estate itself. Those wines traditionally produced at Mount Palomar include Chardonnay, Reserve Chardonnay, Cabernet Sauvignon, Sirah, Viognier and Sangiovese. A Port is made from Petite Sirah and Zinfandel grapes, a Cream Sherry from Palomino grapes.

The winery and tasting room are located at 33820 Rancho California Road in the center of the Temecula Wine Country.

The Chardonnay is barrel fermented using several types of yeast for complexity of flavors. Through extensive leaf removal to insure improved air circulation and vine hedging, Mount Palomar has been able to enhance the fruit qualities of the wines bearing their attractive logos.

Beginning in 1982 when he became the winery's Operations Manager, Peter Poole has developed new packaging and label designs, created new brands for the winery and spearheaded vari-

etal changes in both the vineyards and the wines produced. During that time, Poole has served for three terms as president of the Temecula Valley Vintners Association in addition to serving as a member of the Regional Representatives Council and as a board member of the Wine Institute, the industry's professional advisory body.

Today, Peter Poole oversees the entire operations of Mount Palomar Winery, working closely with Winemaker Etienne Cowper and Vineyard Manager Vidal Perez to guarantee uncompromised quality to consumers of the winery's products. Eight members of the Poole family share ownership in Mount Palomar, while the third generation, Peter's two sons and a daughter, has already made contributions in the wine cellars, tasting room, shipping department, label design and public relations. The family and staff are responsible for a number of special events that have become

This distinctive label identifies Mount Palomar's Rey Sol line of Rhone-style varietal wines.

increasingly popular with local residents and others visiting the facility. A Spring Vineyard Walk, Candlelight Barrel Tasting and Winemaker Dinners are among these festive celebrations.

Since its inception, Mount Palomar has been dedicated to researching the best methods for Temecula vineyards and has commercially grown more than twenty grape varieties. In addition, an equal number of separate varieties have been tested from experimental vineyard plots. While the vineyard also supplies neighboring Temecula wineries with varietal grapes, the facility is capable of growing from a current production of fifteen thousand cases to an annual production of twenty-five thousand cases, while using only estate-grown grapes. Recent years have brought about a change in Mount Palomar's grape production, as Peter Poole has begun to focus production away from traditional wines of Northern California to the classic wines of the Mediterranean region. Since a look at a globe quickly reveals the geographic similarity of the Temecula Valley to the Mediterranean regions of France, Spain and Italy, it is logical that Southern European varietal grapes might well thrive here and produce outstanding new wines to provide the wine-drinking public with something new to savor.

In Central Italy's Tuscany, wines made from the classic Sangiovese grape are considered among the nation's top red varieties. Those known as "Super Tuscans" are comprised of an exclusive group made from high quality limited yields aged in small oak barrels, similar in style to the quality wines of France and California. Mount Palomar's Castelletto Sangiovese is produced in this manner. The name "Castelletto" honors Peter Poole's mother's family, and has been the recipient of numerous awards since introduction of the line in 1991 with the release of that year's Sangiovese. The blend is primarily the varietal itself with an additional per-

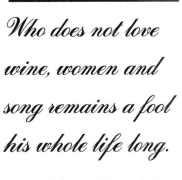

Who does not love wine, women and song remains a fool his whole life long.

-- *Johann Heinrich Voss*

centage of other varieties to match the Chianti Classico style of Italy. It was named "The Best Wine of the South Coast Region" at a recent California State Fair.

Another award-winning wine of the Castelletto series has been Mount Palomar's Cortese, made from a highly regarded white grape of Northern Italy's Piemonte region. It's traditionally Italy's most expensive white wine, with a distinctive fruit flavor. Estate bottled from the winery's vineyards, it was named the "Best Pacific Rim White" at another recent international wine competition. The winery also produces other Mediterranean-style wines like Syrah and Rhone varietals and blends made from from pioneer vineyards in the nearby Cucamonga Valley. Recent plantings in Mount Palomar's vineyards include white Rhone varieties such as Roussanne, Marsanne and Viognier.

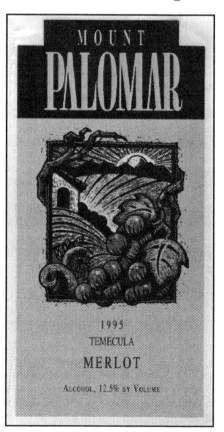

Mount Palomar's Merlot wine has won many awards.

About the Winemaker

When Etienne Paul Cowper was named Mount Palomar's winemaker prior to the 1991 harvest, the winery gained an experienced professional with an impressive background in the field. He's a native of nearby Orange County and earned his undergraduate degree in Cultural Anthropology from California State University Fullerton, eventually going north to California State University Fresno to complete a Master's Degree (with distinction) in Agricultural Chemistry within the Enology Program, and was recipient of a Graduate Program Award in the department.

Internships with various California wineries culminated with an assignment following graduation at the prestigious Konocti Winery in Lake County. In subsequent years as Konocti's winemaker, his wines won thirty-five major awards, including fifteen Gold, Platinum and Best of Show honors. His next assignment was as Senior Assistant Winemaker/Enologist at the celebrated Kendall Jackson Winery in Lakeport, where he supervised a variety of successful projects.

His experiences in Northern California provided him with opportunities to work closely with a number of legendary winemakers including John Parducci, Jed Steele and Andre Tchelitscheff. Knowledge of his success was not unnoticed at Mount Palomar, and he joined the Poole family's team of viticulturists and winemakers in 1991. Since then, he's traveled exensively to Italy and Southern France to broaden his knowledge of Mediterranean style wines.

In spite of his French-sounding surname, Etienne Cowper is all-American and dedicated to a personalized and handcrafted approach to winemaking.

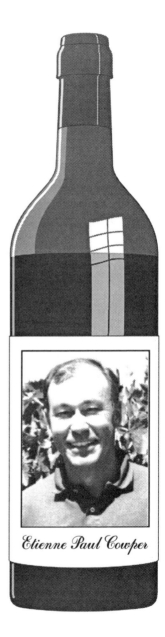

Etienne Paul Cowper

Son Bill and Winemaker Joe Hart share duties at their family winery.

Hart Winery

J oe Travis Hart and his wife, Nancy, are proud to display the numerous ribbons and awards their family's winery has accumulated since the first vintage they produced bearing the Hart label was released in 1980.

They had purchased twelve acres of hillside land in 1973 and planted the initial acre of varietal grapes the following year. Today, the small but successful Hart Winery annually makes and bottles more than four thousand cases of a wide range of premium wines, and plans are under way to increase production to meet the growing demand for their distinctive wines.

A native of Holtville, California, Joe engaged in several careers following college, including teaching junior high school and working on oceanography at Scripps Institution in La Jolla. Son of an early aviator, he owns and flies a 1953 Cessna 170B, a classic taildragger.

Joe was an avid home winemaker when he decided to join those who shared his belief that the Temecula Valley was destined to join other California regions with a microclimate ideal for producing quality wines.

Beginning in 1974, planting increased as Joe and his family added new varieties and grafted over some of the original vines to those with anticipated potential to add to the winery's line.

The acreage has expanded over the years and is currently planted in Sauvignon Blanc, Syrah,

1996
SYRAH
TEMECULA, CALIFORNIA

PRODUCED AND BOTTLED BY HART WINERY
TEMECULA, CALIFORNIA • ALCOHOL 13.5% BY VOLUME

This Hart wine has won more than its share of connoisseurs' approval.

Semillon, Cabernet Franc, Barbera, Merlot and Viognier. To meet the needs of marketing, additional grapes are purchased from nearby Temecula Valley vineyards, as well as from old-vine vineyards in the historic Cucamonga Valley, where the warmer climate is beneficial to the production of such popular Southern Rhone Valley varietals as Cinsault, Grenache and Mourvedre.

While the enterprise is not exactly a one-man operation, Joe Hart personally oversees each and every phase of the winemaking process from the cultivation of the vines through final bottling and labeling of the wines that bear his family's name.

The Hart Winery isn't reluctant to experiment

with blends and grapes others have yet to discover. Their Bordeaux-style blends of Cabernet Franc and Merlot and another blend of Semillon and Sauvignon Blanc as well as a Southern Rhone type combining Grenache, Mourvedre, Cinsault and Syrah grapes have each received accolades from those preferring wines made in the European fashion. In recent years, the winery has released in extremely limited quantities a fortified dessert wine produced from the rare Italian Aleatico grape.

While Joe Hart serves as winemaker and viticulturist, his son, Bill, has taken on additional responsibilities in recent years as assistant winemaker.

During the hectic weeks of bottling the annual vintage, Nancy Hart and other family members, along with volunteers, take turns at the winery in various capacities to ensure an uninterrupted flow of wines. On occasions, the Harts assist other growers in bottling limited editions of special label wines.

The winery itself is located on a scenic estate north of Rancho California Road near the entrance to the Wine Country at 41300 Avenida Biona. A dirt road leads to a quaint structure housing both the winery and a small tasting area and a warehouse storing finished wines. A tasting fee of $3 includes an attractive souvenir wine glass and the opportunity to chat with either the winemaker or a member of his staff while sampling several varietal wines.

While picnicking facilities are limited and food is not available, the winery participates in many of the special activities planned by the region's Temecula Valley Vintners Association, including barrel tastings and the annual New/Nouveau Wine samplings.

The winery is open daily from 9 a.m. to 4:30 p.m. for tasting, and the public is always welcome to visit. Tours are available upon request. A call

Let us have wine and women, mirth and laughter, sermons and soda water the day after.

-- Lord Byron

to 676-6300 will reveal details of special upcoming events.

The Southern Rhone Valley's varietal grapes are represented in Hart's Viognier wine.

Meet the Winemaker

Joe Travis Hart's usual attire as he attends to the needs of his Hart Winery is a blue denim shirt and jeans. He not only looks the part of a winemaker, but also carries out this role with expertise as well as aplomb.

His background as an educator, oceanographer, pilot and winemaker would make him fit the description of a Renaissance Man, and those who get to know him agree that his demeanor and charm make him a sought-after companion. His red wines have gathered numerous ribbons and awards, and his willingness to share his knowledge with others is responsible for his many friends in the wine industry. He seems never too busy to chat with those who seek his wisdom, even when tasks at hand demand his professional attention. A visit to his modest winery when he isn't out toiling among the vines is an experience not to be missed.

Don't let his Santa-like beard and shock of white hair fool you! He's young at heart and both enthusiastic and optimistic about the future of each year's vintage.

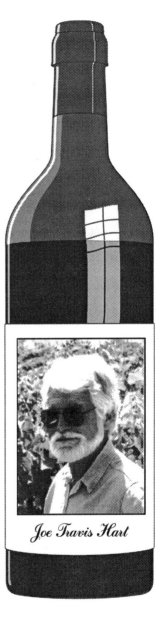

Joe Travis Hart

41

*Dr. Bill Filsinger and his wife Kathy pose in their cozy tasting room
and display Kathy's distinctive champagne bottle design.*

42

Filsinger Vineyards & Winery

Boris Pasternak's poetic *Dr. Zhivago* wasn't the only physician to have interests away from medicine. Dr. Robin Cook is an accomplished novelist as is the creator of *E.R.* and *Jurassic Park*, Dr. Michael Crichton. In the Temecula Valley, Dr. Bill Filsinger has made a name for himself as an award-winning winemaker and viticulturist since he retired from his successful medical practice in 1997.

These days Dr. Filsinger has exchanged his lab coat for blue jeans has become Winemaker Bill Filsinger and, along with his wife, Kathy, owns and operates Filsinger Vineyards & Winery. The couple purchased thirty-five acres from Martha Daniels in 1974 and, as the grapes they planted thrived, they opened their own winery six years later.

Following medical school and a tour of duty as a flight surgeon in the U.S. Air Force, Dr. Filsinger opened his practice in Southern California. His parents had been winemakers in the Heidelberg and Mainz regions in Germany and came to America prior to World War II. The family heritage was such that the prospect of becoming a winemaker was always in the back of his mind, and became a reality as a result of the acquisition of the De Portola parcel. Initially, he planted three varietals, Zinfandel, Sauvignon Blanc and Chardonnay and later added additional acreage in Gewurztraminer and Cabernet Sauvignon. When these produced sufficient grapes, he sold the crop to other area wineries. It wasn't until 1980 that his first release under the Filsinger label was marketed, and this was honored with a gold medal at the Orange County Fair competition.

Today, the Filsingers' youngest son, Eric, serves as cellarmaster and assists his father in the day-to-day winemaking chores at the site. Approximately ninety percent of estate-grown grapes are used in the winery's production, with the remaining ten percent obtained from other Temecula vineyards.

Dr. Filsinger is more likely to be found in his winery rather than in a medical office these days.

Filsinger was the first Temecula winemaker to produce an estate-grown Gewurztraminer, a spicy Alsatian wine similar to that produced by has ancestral family in Germany. Many consider this to be an ideal complement to Oriental cuisine, as the wine's tangy flavor isn't overpowered by the food's often pungent seasoning.

Other still wines made at the winery include the original Sauvignon Blanc and Zinfandel, now produced in a lowered-alcohol White Zin style, blended with a very small percentage of Gewurztraminer or Sauvignon Blanc.

Fumé Blanc, Nebbiolo, and Cabernet Sauvignon round out their varietal listing, with the Cab considered by many to be top of their line. Once in a while, the winemaker releases a wine with a "Special Reserve" designation on the label. While it may be the practice in some instances for wines grown in other regions to use this term rather loosely, Filsinger doesn't play this game. The doctor holds back wines he feels will improve with aging and only permits release when he's convinced the ideal time has arrived. This took place in both 1993 and 1997. Filsinger wines are now marketed and distributed to such diverse locations as Japan, Scotland and England.

When asked whether he considers wine to be a food or a beverage, he replies, "Neither a food nor a beverage. Wine is actually a condiment, and when poured with a complementing dish, serves to improve both the taste and the enjoyment of that repast."

What sets the Filsinger Vineyards and Winery aside from many others is the reputation they have enjoyed in the production of sparkling wines, starting in 1986. Filsinger employs the traditional French *méthode champenoise* style, and the words "Fermented in this bottle" appear on the distinctive labels. While some wineries sell sparkling wines that have been produced elsewhere, a close look

Filsinger's Special Reserve Cabernet Sauvignon is termed "the wine of the century" by the winmaker.

at the packaging will usually reveal that the production of the "champagne" took place at another location, frequently at Mission San Jose or similar bulk source. Dr. Filsinger is proud to tell the consumer world that his grapes come from Temecula and the bubbly is produced in the time-honored process. Dr. Filsinger claims there's no adequate substitute for the painstaking and time-consuming classic method, developed some three centuries ago by the legendary French monk, Dom Perignon. It's a lengthy procedure from harvest to release, but to hear the winemaker describe the necessary and traditional steps, it's well worth the requisite effort.

"First we harvest the targeted Chardonnay grapes earlier than those we'll later crush for our still wines," he explains. "That's because we want to hold down the sugar level while still maintaining the characteristics of the varietal grapes.

"Following the crush, yeast is added and the primary fermentation process is under way. When we've achieved the levels of sugar and alcohol we desire, then we add *liquor de tirage* in the form of cane sugar as well as another yeast culture, and bottle the resultant blend with temporary caps."

The second fermentation of this cuveé may take up to five years, depending upon the style of sparkling wine to be made. This is the time that the effervescence that characterizes champagne develops.

Filsinger's Brut Natural spends five years or longer on yeast, while the Diamond Cuvee spends three.

The next step is the traditional "riddling" process. A process tilts and rotates each bottle on a regular schedule to force sediments down to the bottle's neck. Each bottle may be riddled as often as a hundred times during the several weeks it takes to complete this vital act.

Vintage 1997
TEMECULA

Nebbiolo

PRODUCED AND BOTTLED BY
FILSINGER VINEYARDS & WINERY, INC.
TEMECULA, CALIFORNIA USA
BW CA NO.4959 ALCOHOL 12.2% BY VOLUME

Filsinger's Nebbiolo is another favorite at the tasting room.

To remove the yeast and grape sediments that have collected, the bottle neck is frozen to an ice plug in a special ice-cold brine solution to remove the cap. The carbon dioxide that's formed inside helps to disgorge the plug. Depending on the style of sparkling wine desired, the cellarmaster adds a calibrated dosage of sugar blended with the original wine to refill the bottle.

"It takes a great deal of time and effort, of course." Dr. Filsinger adds, "but there's no alternate way to produce classic champagnes. We wouldn't want it any other way."

Filsinger's premium sparkling wines are available in three styles. The most popular selections for weddings is known as "Diamond Cuveé," and as Filsinger is known to have remarked, "Diamonds are a girl's best friend." It's produced from the Chardonnay grape and aged in oak.

Filsinger's Brut Natural Blanc de Blanc is also produced from Chardonnay grapes with five years on yeast. It's the driest of the cellar's sparkling wines. Its distinctive formal label was designed by Kathy Filsinger.

A Brut Rosé made from the Gamay grape has a distinctive characteristic and isn't quite as dry as the Brut Natural. Each has its own characteristic and is released only when the winemaker and cellarmaster agree it's at the ideal time for consumption.

The cozy tasting room is located at 39050 De Portola Road, in Temecula. Both indoor and outdoor meeting facilities are available to accommodate up to fifty individuals, with advance reservations required. A covered picnic area and light snacks are available to visitors on weekends from 10:00 a.m. to 5 p.m. and on Friday afternoons, 11 a.m. to 4 p.m. Tours of the adjacent winery may be arranged. There is a $1 charge for tasting and additional information may be obtained by calling 676-4594.

> *"Time spent without a glass of wine is time wasted."*
>
> --Albert Einstein

48

About the Winemaker

Those who have been medical patients of Dr. Bill Filsinger during his long and successful career as a physician and surgeon know of his careful and caring personality, He has transferred these characteristics to his new vocation, and it is apparent to those who enjoy his carefully crafted wines that he is personally responsible for each and every step in their production.

With wife Kathy and son Eric, the Filsingers have enjoyed an enviable reputation as active members of the Temecula Valley wine family. Whether carrying out the mundane tasks of keeping up with the winemaking process or pouring their premium varietal wines at various charity and tasting events, the Filsingers have earned the right to be proud of the wines bearing their distinctive labels.

While off the beaten track, a visit to the Filsinger Winery is always a rewarding experience and well worth the drive to 39050 De Portola Road.

Dr. Bill Filsinger

This beautiful Victorian-style showplace is the home of the Van Roekel family's Maurice Car'rie Winery.

Maurice Car'rie Winery

When the Van Roekel family moved to Temecula Valley in 1984, they were planning to enjoy some leisure time after a busy career involving the ownership and management of a number of roller skating rinks and the design and manufacture of custom wheels. It wasn't long, however, before they discovered the region's expanding wine industry and decided to begin a new and exciting chapter in their colorful lives.

They had operated the popular "Skate Ranch" in neighboring Orange County since 1955 when Caltrans announced plans to construct a new freeway complex adjacent to their Santa Ana property. Soon the word was out that future projections for the immediate area included a major shopping mall to be known as "Main Place." Seeing the writing on the wall, G. Budd and Maurice Car'rie Van Roekel decided the time was ripe to take advantage of the opportunity to spend more time with their grandchildren and perhaps invest in a citrus or avocado grove. After all, they were well aware of the fact that the Temecula Valley boasted a unique climate conducive to agriculture. The prospect of being a "gentleman farmer" appealed to Budd's venturesome side.

But avocados and citrus lost out when he learned of the availability of a forty-six acre vineyard in the Temecula Valley. It had been planted in 1968 as the first vineyard in the region and had provided grapes for other area wineries established in the interim. All it lacked was a winery, and the Van Roekel family remedied that deficiency quickly with the design and construction of a distinctive Victorian-style architectural showplace. They took advantage of the site's original windmill and land-scaped it with hundreds of blooming rose bushes. There's an adjacent gazebo, and new additions including a banquet room and veranda.

Naming the new enterprise was no challenge for the Van Roekel family as they selected "Maurice Car'rie" for their winery's title, in honor of the co-owner's first and middle names. Budd Van Roekel serves as president of the winery, while his wife functions as both secretary and media contact.

The original forty-six acres purchased in 1984 encompasses 120 acres with twenty more soon to be planted. Production has increased to the point that the winery is responsible for twenty-five thou-

Budd and Maurice Car'rie Van Roekel are partners in life as well as in their wineries.

-- *Kirk S. Irwin*

VINTAGE 1997
TEMECULA

Muscat Canelli

ALCOHOL 11.6% BY VOLUME

Maurice Car'rie's Muscat Canelli is a popular dessert wine.

sand cases of premium varietal wine, and plans are under way to expand to thirty-three thousand in the near future.

The vineyards originally produced only two varietal grapes: Chenin Blanc and Sauvignon Blanc, but these have been augmented to the point that Cabernet Sauvignon, Cabernet Blanc, White Zinfandel, two Chardonnays, Merlot, Petite Sirah, Johannisberg Riesling, Muscat Canelli, Gamay Rosé, Gamay Beaujolais Nouveau and a Late Harvest Riesling now all bear the colorful Maurice Car'rie label. Additional proprietary wines bear the names of the Van Roekel grandchildren: Heather's Mist, Cody's Crush, Sara Bella and Summer's End. There is also a Collage occasionally produced by the winery when the component wines are judged to be of the required caliber to meet the winemaker's requirements. It is a blend of Cabernet Franc, Petite Sirah and Merlot and is reminiscent of the premium wines of classic French chateaux.

CHARMAT METHOD SPARKLING WINE; SECONDARY FERMENTATION BEFORE BOTTLING

2000

Turn of the *Century*

Maurice Car'rie

— *California Champagne* —

ALCOHOL 11% BY VOLUME

Maurice Car'rie celebrates the turn of the century with this California champagne.

Visitors to the Maurice Car'rie Winery are welcome from 10 a.m. to 5 p.m. daily, and conducted tours may be arranged by appointment only. Visitors may sample four to five different wines poured from a list that is changed weekly.

The winery is located at 34225 Rancho California Road and features a gift shop stocked with an extensive selection of wine memorabilia and colorful ideas for wine-related gift items. The picnic area and lawns that surround the winery's entrance are ideal for leisurely enjoying Maurice Car'rie wines while snacking on deli-type foods available from the tasting room. The phone number there is 676-1711.

Weekend activities are planned throughout the year with big band sounds, barn dances, art, flower and car shows among the featured events.

Meet the Winemaker

Mike Tingley wears two hats—he serves as winemaker at both the Maurice Car'rie and Van Roekel Wineries. Since each is owned and operated by the Van Roekel family, this proves to have no real conflicts of interest, but it does call upon his energies and time during the busy crush each year.

A native of Anaheim in neighboring Orange County, Mike started out to be a professional musician and had a successful career in the Netherlands under way when he discovered the joys of European wines and returned to California to learn the fine points of making wine himself.

Classes from the University of California Davis and an apprenticeship at Callaway as a lab technician, at Cilurzo as a winemaker and now Maurice Car'rie have provided him with a wide range of experiences working with the wines of the Temecula Valley.

He claims his goal as a winemaker is to be able to "fully express the potential of the Temecula fruit" to which he has access. Judging from the awards his wines have won since his appointment as Car'rie and Van Roekel winemaker in March of 1995, he seems well on the way to meeting these expectations.

Mike lives in nearby Murrieta with his wife and two sons and says he is especially proud of his Nouveau wines.

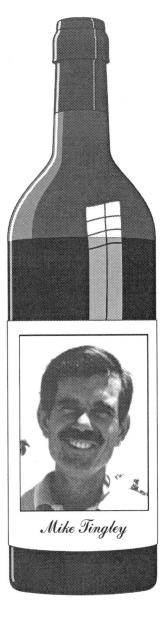

Mike Tingley

Phil and Carol Baily are the winemakers at both Baily Vineyard & Winery and Temecula Crest Winery. They describe their winemaking philosophy as follows, "We like wines which highlight the character of the fruit; which are clean and crisp with intense aroma and bouquet. To accomplish this, we pick the grapes at optimum ripeness and let the wines literally make themselves, intervening in the natural process as little as possible."

Baily Vineyard & Winery

In 1981 Phil and Carol Baily were living in San Marino where they were active home winemakers, acquiring grapes wherever they could be found. That year the couple purchased a home and acreage on a hillside site on Pauba Road in Temecula, where they planted a single acre in varietal grapes the following year. Another year went by, and the Bailys planted an additional six acres. By then they had both taken extension courses in Enology at the University of California Davis and knew their dream of owning and operating their own winery and producing a very small quantity of premium wines was within reach.

Phil's consulting business continued to occupy much of his time, and now he and Carol were faced with the added responsibility of designing and constructing a modern facility for producing and storing an increasing volume of wine. By 1986, the Baily Vineyard & Winery became a reality and its distinctive label became the newest to bear the Temecula appellation.

Those visiting local wineries enjoyed their tour of the new facility, and word of mouth helped to direct weekend visitors to the attractive tasting room located above the stored barrels of aging Baily wines.

Connoisseurs agreed with judges of major wine adjudications that a small new winery with a talented staff could compete with much larger and

Baily

1998

temecula

white riesling-dry

bottled by Baily Winery Temecula, California
alcohol 11.9% by volume ;residual sugar 0.8% by weight
contains sulfites

Baily wines have captured numerous awards and compliments from judges.

better-known operations

Baily wines received recognition at all of the prestigious California wine judgings, including the California State Fair, the San Francisco Fair, the Orange County Fair, the Riverside County National Wine Competition, the Los Angeles County Fair, the New World International Wine Competition and the San Diego National Wine Competition. Production had to be increased, even though the wines were at the time in very limited distribution.

A Chardonnay, White Riesling, Dry Riesling, Cabernet Blanc, Muscat Blanc, Merlot, Blush Cabernet, Cabernet Sauvignon and Late Harvest Riesling were soon produced, along with a Sauvignon Blanc and Semillon blend known as

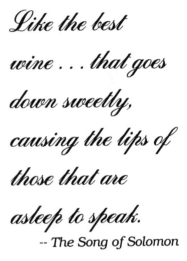

"Montage." Unique to the Baily line is a proprietary blend, a light-bodied fruity wine made from Cabernet Sauvignon known as "TV Red" The TV stands for Temecula Valley, of course.

Over the years, Baily's vineyards have increased dramatically in size and now encompass sixty acres of varietal grapes. The majority of wines produced are estate grown, and additional grapes are purchased from neighboring vineyards when the need arises.

Carol Baily is deeply involved in all aspects of the family's business and conducts "Dinners in the Winery." She designs the menu to complement Baily wines and prepares the gourmet meals. In recent years, these popular dinners have led to the family's branching out and opening the Baily Wine Country Café in Temecula. Serving California and Continental cuisine, the restaurant has rapidly become a gathering place for both local residents and visitors to the wine country to enjoy casually elegant dining. Son Christopher Baily is the manager and also carries on an active catering business. It's located in the Temecula Town Center at the corner of Rancho California and Ynez Roads. Reservations are always recommended, and the telephone number is 676-9567.

Because the original tasting room at the winery on Pauba Road quickly became unable to accommodate increasing numbers of visitors, the Bailys are now in the process of opening a new and larger facility on Rancho California Road, in the midst of one of their vineyards. The tasting room is open seven days a week from 10 a.m. to 5 p.m. There is a $4 charge for sampling five Baily wines, and a wine glass is included as a colorful souvenir. Because production is limited, Baily wines are currently available only at the tasting room.

Like the best wine . . . that goes down sweetly, causing the lips of those that are asleep to speak.

-- The Song of Solomon

The distinctive French chateau design of the Thornton Winery on Rancho California Road greets visitors to Temecula's Wine Country .

Thornton Winery

Traveling down Rancho California Road at the gateway of the Temecula Valley Wine Country, the first structure one observes on the right is the French-Mediterranean chateau that is the Thornton Winery. The imposing structure not only houses the award-winning winery and wine storage tanks, but also features a gourmet restaurant as well as an outdoor patio and stage that is the venue of a series of contemporary jazz concerts eight months of the year.

Opened in 1981 in nearby Fallbrook as the Culbertson Winery, the Thornton Winery now annually produces some forty thousand cases of premium varietal wines and a wide range of sparkling wines made in the classic *methode champenoise* tradition. The current Temecula vineyards were planted in 1987, and the winery prides itself in selecting additional grapes from the finest viticultural areas in California to expand its line of varietal wines. These are grown both in neighboring Temecula vineyards and in other appropriate sites within the Golden State's South Coast appellation.

The location of the winery is designed to take advantage of the topography of the hillside environment and view of the verdant valley below. With a steady stream of tourists and wine enthusiasts visiting daily for wine tastings, tours, special events and the popular Café Champagne, ample parking space was set aside in the original plans. Underground caves provide a cool locale for the storage and aging of both still and sparkling wines. A well-stocked gift shop with numerous unusual wine-related items is adjacent to a glassed in area where one might view the ongoing activities of this modern winery.

Wines bearing the distinctive Thornton label reflect both the praised California varietals and those indigenous to the Italian Mediterranean region. The latter include Moscato, Viognier, Cabernet Sauvignon, Merlot, Aleatico and Carignane as well as Cote Red, a blend of Mourvedre, Grenache, Syrah, Cinsault and Terret Noir.

Winemaker Jon McPherson is responsible for the outstanding wines produced by Thornton. In

Thornton Winemaker Jon McPherson takes a personal interest in the progress of the winery's sparkling wines.

Champagne lovers have made this California sparkling wine a favorite.

his words, "My goal for our wines is to create premium varietals from a special selection of grapes grown in the finest California vineyards, using different vinification techniques and barrel aging."

His traditional California varietals are usually released in limited editions and include Coastal Reserve Chardonnay, Pinot Blanc and Zinfandel.

Thornton's principal claim to fame, however, may be in the winery's line of sparkling wines. The winery's sparkling wines have consistently been awarded medals for excellence during recent years, garnering numerous awards and medals. Five of these are currently available. They are the Brut Reserve, a non-vintage Brut, a Blanc de Noir, a Cuveé Rouge and a Cuveé de Frontignan. In May of 1996, Thornton Winery began labeling its premium vintage champagne with an elegant gold medallion and ribboned packaging featuring the celebrated 1985 vintage.

The winery is owned by John M. and Sally B. Thornton, who are among Southern California's most honored civic and business leaders. He holds an M.B.A. degree from the Harvard Business

John and Sally Thornton proudly cradle a bottle of their celebrated sparkling wine.

School while his wife is the recipient of an M.A. in History from the University of San Diego. In addition, he serves on numerous boards including the San Diego Zoological Society for more than twenty years. The Thorntons are also the recipients of numerous awards in recognition of their commitment to the medical and cultural strength of their community. They are active participants in the special events, winemaker dinners and jazz concerts hosted by the Thornton Winery.

This Temecula winery is one of the very few in the United States to feature an epicurean restaurant on its premises, as the Café Champagne continues to win prestigious awards from the Southern California Restaurant Writers. Steve Pickell serves as executive chef over this exciting and much-admired dining experience, featuring fresh seasonal dishes designed to complement

Thornton's varietal wines. These gourmet meals are served in an ambiance of French Country elegance by a dedicated staff of professionals.

As would be expected from a setting as exquisite as Thornton's, numerous weddings, company and family parties and special events are scheduled each month, taking advantage of the champagne lounge, banquet room and Café Champagne. Conferences and other private meetings can be catered with prior advance notice. A telephone call to the winery at 699-3021 will provide details of upcoming Champagne Jazz events as well as other specially scheduled festive seasonal and holiday events.

The Thornton tasting bar is open from 11 a.m. to 4 p.m. daily with a $6 per person charge for four wines. Guided tours take place on weekends only from 12 noon to 4 p.m. on the hour with a tasting following. Café Champagne is open daily from 11 a.m. to 9 p.m. with a contemporary cuisine prepared under Executive Chef Steve Pickell's personal supervision. Information regarding Thornton's exclusive Reserve Club may be ob-

This Mediterranean blend is another of Jon McPherson's newer award-winning releases.

tained by calling (800) 966-0099, while general details of the winery itself should be directed to 699-0099.

Thornton Winery is located at 32575 Rancho California Road in Temecula, four miles to the east of Highway 15.

Premium varietal wines are grown in the vineyards surrounding the Thornton Winery

About the Winemaker

Jon McPherson is somewhat of an outsider when it comes to California winemakers. He's a native Texan whose father, a professor emeritus in the Department of Chemistry at Texas Tech University, helped found the Texas Grape Growers Association and was active in the growth of the state's wine industry. While still involved in the family's wine business, Jon graduated from Texas Tech with a major in food technology and a minor in chemistry. He was recruited to California in 1985 because of his interest in the process of producing sparkling wine and was named Thornton's winemaker in 1987.

It's McPherson's belief that his cuveés should showcase the specific characteristics of varietal grapes included in the blend. While each has its features, the style of winemaking may differ in order to take advantage of the grapes' properties. Every bottle is the result of years of study, experimentation and dedication to the fine art of premium winemaking. He's especially interested in producing sparkling wines that are striking for their freshness and bursts of flavor.

While award-winning sparkling wines were Jon's initial claim to fame, in recent years his still wines have served not only to expand the Thornton inventory, but also have brought accolades from both consumers and his peers among the winemaking profession.

Jon McPherson

This cedar structure greets visitors to the Temecula Crest Tasting Room and Winery.

Temecula Crest Winery

Phil and Carol Baily, not content with one winery, in 1992 formed a partnership to acquire what is now Temecula Crest Winery. Located on a hilltop in the heart of the wine country, the site boasts a 180-degree view of the widespread Temecula Valley.

The vineyard itself was originally planted in 1975 in varietal grapes and in 1984, Bob and Debbie Britton built a winery on the site called Britton Cellars. The thirteen and a half acre site changed hands over the years until Phil and Carol, along with a number of wine-loving local business and professional people, decided to purchase it and establish Temecula Crest. These enthusiasts have taken advantage of their business and professional experiences and, together with Phil and Carol's demonstrated expertise as entrepreneurs, have created a winery with a character all its own and an annual production of thirty-five hundred cases of varietal wines.

It's not unusual on weekends to meet these active partners as they take part in the various tasks that keep a winery operational. Some participate in the actual crushing of the vineyard's grapes, some spend time pouring samples in the attractive tasting room, while others may assist with the myriad routine tasks associated with any such cooperative venture.

The Bailys' background as amateur winemakers, business management advisors and

1997
TEMECULA
CABERNET BLANC

ALCOHOL 11.9% BY VOLUME

This "blanc de noir" is a popular Temecula Crest wine.

successful premium wine producers has served to make this fairly recent addition to the Temecula scene a memorable wine experience for both tourists and visitors from nearby communities.

Among the wines produced by Temecula Crest in recent years are Chardonnay, Cabernet Sauvignon, Sauvignon Blanc, White Riesling, Cabernet Blanc, Merlot, Nebbiolo, Late Harvest Sauvignon Blanc, Muscat Blanc and a proprietary blend termed "Rancho Red." The White Riesling is sold in a lovely cobalt blue bottle and the Muscat Blanc in a frosted container.

Some ninety percent of all wine produced at

Temecula Crest is from their own properties, and the remaining ten percent comes from neighboring Temecula vineyards. While the majority of wine bearing the distinctive Temecula Crest label is only available for tasting and sale at the winery itself, an increasing amount is appearing on retail shelves and is being poured in area restaurants.

Carol Baily periodically prepares gourmet dinners served in the Temecula Crest Barrel Room. Each course is matched with a different Temecula Crest varietal wine to demonstrate the fact that certain wines ideally complement specific dishes. The winery also hosts "Jazz on the Green" concerts that feature popular jazz recording artists and tasty barbecue dinners. VIP tours and tastings for groups of twenty or more can easily be arranged.

Temecula Crest's flavorful Nebbiolo is available at the tasting room and at Baily's Wine Country Cafe.

Seating at these outdoor events is made even more notable when one takes in the delightful panoramic view of Temecula Valley scenery while sipping one of the winery's premium wines and listening to contemporary American jazz.

The winery's tasting room is located in an attractive cedar-faced structure that also houses the day-to-day operations of making, aging and bottling premium varietal wines. Four tastings include a souvenir glass and are available for $4. The winery is open from 12 noon. to 5 p.m. daily and 10 a.m. to 5 p.m. weekends, and there is a large picnic area on the site.

The ambiance at Temecula Crest Winery is, above all, casual, and those who take the time to travel to 40620 Calle Contento, approximately five miles east of the junction of Interstate 15 and Rancho California Road will find the experience both friendly and rewarding.

A special feature of both the Baily and Temecula Crest Wineries is the opportunity to enroll in the Baily & Temecula Crest Wine & Food Club with numerous benefits and fun for members, including discounts on wines, gift items, dinners and lodging. A call to 676-8231 will provide details as well as information regarding Temecula Crest Winery.

About the Winemaker

Steve Hagata ably assists Phil and Carol Baily in the production of Temecula Crest's fine premium wines. Steve's background includes service in other South Coast wineries as well as being the proprietor of his boutique "Las Pietras" Winery located in the Sunshine Summit area off the historic Butterfield Stage Route now known as Highway 79. When he isn't carrying out his responsibilities at Temecula Crest, he heads toward his property north of Warner Springs to care for his own vineyards there. His South Coast Syrah is produced in extremely small quantities, but is rapidly gaining a following.

Steve is particulartly proud of the Cabernet Blanc and Nebbiolo wines produced at the Temecula Crest Winery, and is among those taking bows for the winery's proprietary "Rancho Red" wine.

With his movie star appearanace and genial personality, he's always available to answer wine buff's questions when visiting Temecula Crest. That is, unless he's busily engaged in quality control work or sampling his own products!

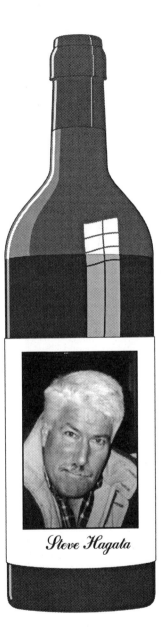

Steve Hagata

73

Barrett Bird operates a "one man winery" in Temecula's wine country.

Santa Margarita Winery

It was 1974 that Barrett H. Bird first planted his four acres in the Temecula Valley in primarily Cabernet Sauvignon grapes, with a few rows of Semillon. At the time, reds dominated the retail wine trade, and he had visions of selling his crop to local wineries in the marketplace that was just beginning to develop.

His prior career had focused on Southern California's aerospace industry, following a period in World War II, in which he'd served as a pilot ferrying war planes for later use in combat. When he eventually retired from the Farr Company in 1979, he had little knowledge of the art of winemaking, let along a degree in viticulture. He just wanted to grow grapes and take the role of a knowledgable amateur.

A man of conviction and dedication, he initially had no desire to become a boutique winemaker, since his limited property situated off a dusty dirt road in rural Temecula was hardly the location to compete with the many wineries popping up along Rancho California Road.

Over a period of several years, he built a twelve hundred square-foot structure that now houses his winemaking operation and minimal tasting facility. In 1991 Santa Margarita released its initial vintage with five hundred gallons of 1985 estate grown and bottled Cabernet Sauvignon wine. Since then, the total annual production has grown to just under a thousand cases, still a drop in the

75

> *Wine is the drink of the gods, milk the drink of babies, tea the drink of women, and water the drink of beasts.*
>
> —*John Stuart Blackie*

barrel when compared to neighboring Temecula wineries.

The winery and tasting room are closed to the public from July to October so that Bird can over-see the complicated efforts of the crush and other labors in the vineyard. Those wishing to visit must do so on Saturdays and Sundays. His is a small and friendly winery with no corporate ties, sales personnel or advertising. His reputation has been built mainly by word of mouth, and the word is that his Santa Margarita Vineyard & Winery is one that deserves to be visited.

It's not always possible at any of California's legion of wineries to be absolutely certain of the opportunity to chat with the winemaker and viticulturist. Since both at Santa Margarita are in the person of genial Barrett Bird, this is one such place.

The winery is the exclusive site to taste and purchase Santa Margarita wines and, when asked, Bird is pleased to explain how he named his op-eration.

"The Rainbow Gap in the Santa Ana Moun-tain Range to the west was formed by the waters of the Santa Margarita River. If it weren't for that gap in the mountains, then the cool ocean breezes that we enjoy in the evenings might never hit the Temecula Wine Country. That, coupled with the warm air we enjoy during most days, makes up the unique microclimate that helps our grapes mature to their full potential. I thought it would be a good idea to honor that fact."

Bird's Cabernet Sauvignon differs from most others produced locally in that he is content to release only small lots of high quality wines aged in seasoned cooperage for a minimum of four years. He has recently grafted Merlot and Petit Verdot for blending purposes in his continuing search for the perfect marriage of color, bouquet and acid/sugar balance.

VINTAGE 1993

Santa Margarita

Temecula

CONTAINS SULFITES

Cabernet Sauvignon

Red
Table Wine

MADE AND BOTTLED BY SANTA MARGARITA VINEYARD AND WINERY
TEMECULA, CA

In addition to his signature Cabernet, this owner-winemaker grows both Semillon and some Sauvignon Blanc in his vineyard and purchases small amounts of Sauvignon Blanc and other varietals from his neighbors.

The twisted shillelagh on his label is in respect to Barrett Bird's Irish roots.

Barrett Bird's Santa Margarita Winery is located at 33490 Madera de Playa, off Calle Contento. The tasting room is open from 11 a.m. to 4:30 p.m. on weekends from November until sold out, and sampling takes place in the winery's combined warehouse and all-purpose structure three-quarters of a mile west of Calle Contento.

There's a real treat awaiting those who take the time to travel and survive the corrugated dirt road leading to the site, but there's always the chance that a "Sorry, sold out" sign may be tacked to the door.

There's no charge for tasting as long as supplies last, but once the current release is depleted, the winery closes down until after the subsequent year's crush. With no current plans for expansion,

Santa Margarita is content to continue to do what it does best: make it worth the time and patience it takes for a jack-of-all-wine-trades winemaker to practice his craft with both style and love for the grape.

His is the only local tasting room where visitors can have their samples poured by the winemaker himself with bottles and glasses resting on upturned wine barrels.

Both the wines and the accompanying conversations are always memorable.

About the Winemaker

Barrett Bird started out in his San Pedro garage as a home winemaker producing wine in five-gallon glass springwater carboys. He purchased grapes from various sources prior to discovering and investing in the Temecula Valley. His ancestry is Irish, as anyone meeting him for the first time might well discern. While it was several generations back that great-grandfather Charles Barrett emigrated from County Cork in the Emerald Isle to settle in Michigan, his namesake's Gaelic gene pool is reflected in Barrett's appearance and wit. The twisted shillelagh on his simple label is in respect to these Irish roots.

His is the last of the one-man wineries in the valley. While he does employ others to assist with the annual harvest and bottling, it's the multiple tasks of growing grapes and making fine wines that fall to Bird's hands. He's the one who leaves his home early in the morning in a red pick-up truck to select and plant the desired cuttings, and grafts over to new varietals when required. He leaf and cluster prunes and also deals with various varmints and pests, repairs faulty irrigation lines, mows between rows of verdant vines and decides when and if the acid and sugar balance is ideal for the season's crush.

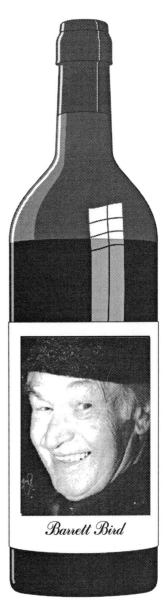

Barrett Bird

-- Kirk S. Irwin

This impressive entry is the initial sight that welcomes Van Roekel Winery visitors.

Van Roekel Vineyard & Winery

Not content to own and operate one of Temecula's largest wineries, the Van Roekel family purchased more than sixty acres in 1988 and added the Van Roekel Vineyard & Winery to the existing and adjacent Maurice Car'rie Winery. The vineyard encompasses 120 acres today and features an attractive wine tasting room complete with extensive gift shop, packaged gourmet foods and beautifully landscaped outdoor picnic area.

At one time the Mesa Verde Winery occupied the site, although those who remember the original grounds would have a difficult time comparing that stark and simple operation with the one that today graces the location.

The initial buildings are now used for storage purposes, while extensive construction and remodeling have transformed the site into a bright and engaging addition to those wineries already making the Temecula Valley a magnet for wine connoisseurs and tourists alike.

The Van Roekel name obviously has antecedence in Holland, and this Dutch heritage is reflected in the massive windmill that serves as a landmark at the winery's colorful entrance. Seasonal flower displays add to the ambiance of one of the newer operations to join the pantheon of premium wineries in the Valley.

The success of the original Maurice Car'rie Winery led husband and wife team of Budd and

Maurice C. Van Roekel to expand its domain to the east in 1989, but it wasn't until 1994 that the tasting room was opened to enthusiastic visitors.

While each of the family's wineries has its own identity, label and varietal wine list, the two share facilities for the actual crushing and fermentation of their grapes at the original Car'rie location.

Wines bearing the Van Roekel Vineyards label include two Chardonnays, Pinot Blanc, Gewurztraminer, White Zinfandel, Muscat Canelli, Mourvedre, Merlot and Cabernet Sauvignon. The two Chardonnays differ in that one is produced in the more traditional manner, while the other is fermented " a boire," and ready to drink.

A Late Harvest Zinfandel was recently added to the winery's selections as well as an occasional Late Harvest Dessert wine with the proprietary des-

May Martin is one of the knowledgable staff serving the Van Roekel tasting room.

These two wines are often requested at the tasting room.

ignation as "Allegria." In all, six thousand cases are produced annually with the distinctive green and gold label.

Van Roekel's varietal grapes are usually harvested during the months of August and September, and the crush itself may take from four to six weeks, depending on climate conditions.

According to Winemaker Mike Tingley, varietal grapes will ripen at different times, and one vine may produce between twenty and forty pounds of grapes.

"We look for a yield of between three and seven tons of grapes from an acre of vines," Tingley says, "and each ton of grapes will yield on an average 720 bottles.

"A single bottle of varietal wine represents approximately three pounds of grapes and the combined efforts of everyone associated with our Van Roekel staff."

These Van Roekel wines can be found on the shelves of retail stores, since sales are no longer

In celebration of the Millennium, Van Roekel provides a special label sparkling wine.

limited to the wine-tasting room at the Temecula winery and several Southern California restaurants. As with the Maurice Car'rie Winery, there is a $2.50 charge for sampling white wines including a souvenir logo glass, and a $5 charge for sampling red wines. The engaging tasting room is open daily from 10 a.m. to 5 p.m., except for Thanksgiving, Christmas and New Year's Day. It features an antique tasting bar where Van Roekel's reds are enjoyed.

"We're looking forward to having our many friends who annually visit our Maurice Car'rie Winery drop in next door and see the newest addition to the family's winemaking ventures," says Budd Van Roekel.

"After all, thousands of guests take part in the tastings, banquets, luncheons and special events we host each year. It's only natural when they're at 34225 Rancho California Road that they'd want to see what's going on up the highway at 34567 and stop by to visit our Van Roekel site."

Those wishing specific information regard-

ing special events, as well as those who have questions regarding the Van Roekel wines, may call
699-6961 during hours the winery is open.

An increasingly popular stop on the Temecula Wine Country Winery
Tour is Keyways' tasting room.

Keyways Winery & Vineyard

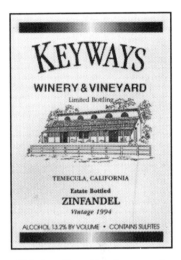

This is a favorite of many of Keyways' visitors.

Carl L. Key established his winery and vineyard in 1990 at 37338 De Portola Road, the third winery to be located away from Rancho California Road in Temecula.

His premium varietal wines, produced or cellared and bottled in Temecula, offer a spectrum of popular consumer types and are available at the attractive tasting room. They include five whites and two reds. The Zinfandel is a favorite of many and is produced on the winemaking estate from vines thought to be forty years old. The other red is a dry Cabernet Sauvignon.

Key's white wines can be sampled in his eclectic tasting room and include Chardonnay, Sauvignon Blanc and White Zinfandel.

The tasting room contains collections ranging from miniature gas lamps to other unusual items and offer visitors the opportunity to browse among them while sampling Keyway's products. A gift shop offers a wide variety of treasures for visitors. There is a modest $1 charge for tasting five of the winery's current releases and the winery is open daily from 10 a.m. to 5 p.m.

The owner serves as winemaster, and questions regarding the winery should be directed to 676-1451.

Stuart Cellars tasting room sits on a hilltop overlooking Rancho California Road.

Stuart Cellars

As one of the Temecula Valley's most recently established wineries, Stuart Cellars began its wine making efforts in 1995 as a result of Marshall Stuart's passion for wine and subsequent studies through the University of California at Davis. He became knowledgable in both enology and viticulture, and then carried out a valuable apprenticeship at Temecula's Keyways Winery. Using the facilities of neighboring established wineries, he began to produce his own wines with the dream of someday opening his own facility. That dream came true on May 15, 1998 with the formal opening of Stuart Cellars at 33515 Rancho California Road, in the heart of Temecula's existing premium wineries.

While serving as a successful general contractor during the week, Marshall Stuart has specialized in grading of both street and governmental projects. His 40 acre estate vineyard will produce its initial crop from the 1999 harvest with vines planted in the French tradition of north to south orientation. According to Stuart, this method serves to give consistency to grapes on both sides of the vines in allowing them to ripen evenly. In addition, at the time the overhead sun is at its highest, the canopy of leaves protects the ripening grapes.

Thirty acres of the Stuart vineyard are devoted to Chardonnay, Merlot and Cabernet Sauvignon.

The remaining acreage is planted in Syrah, Viognier and Zinfandel. At full capacity and maturity of the vines, the vineyard is expected to produce approximately 240 tons of varietal grapes, and yield enough juice to result in some 16,000 cases of premium wine.

It's a family operation at Stuart Cellars, with Marshall Stuart's children taking various expanding roles in the day-to-day activities of the growing business.

Sampling Stuart Cellars products at the winery's tasting room provides four opportunities at $4, and this includes an etched logo glass. Currently, a Chardonnay, Viognier, Zinfandel, Muscat and 100 percent Zinfandel Port are offered from the varietal menu, along with two additional proprietary wines. They are "Callista," a blend of Rhone whites and Sauvignon Blanc, and "Tatria," a blend of Cabernet Sauvignon, Cabernet Franc and Merlot.

Grading is underway at press time for Stuart Cellars' proposed ampitheatre. It's located to the north of the winery tasting room on Rancho California Road. The tasting room is open daily from 10 a.m. to 5 p.m., and the phone number for details is 676-6414.

Stuart Cellars Chardonnay is aged twelve months in New American Oak.

About the Winemaker

It's rare that a winemaker is born into the profession, and Marshall Stuart is no exception to this
rule. With the opening of his family-named winery
in 1998, he finally realized a dream come true.
While he was still managing a profitable business
as a general contractor in Southern California, he
had continued to take classes in enology and
viticulture and was eventually employed part-time
with Temecula's Keyways Winery. He continued to
hone is skills until a suitable acreage became available on Rancho California Road in the midst of
Temecula's growing premium wine country.

Now, his 40 acre estate is a reality and his
varietal wines are gaining the priase of both his
peers and judges at prestigious competitions.

A special feature of the Stuart Cellars is the
winemaker's interest in developing blends of various popular Rhone Valley grapes, with the results
named "Callista" and "Tatria."

His contracting business offers another benefit: Stuart's bulldozers have carvcd out an
ampitheatre among his vines, and this is to be the
site of future concerts and special events.

Marshall Stuart

Jerry Wilson pays individual attention to each of his varietal vines.

Wilson Creek

Thirty years ago in Minnesota, when Gerry and Rosie Wilson made rhubarb and dandelion wines in tubs beside the sauna in their basement, little did they realize that they would one day be constructing a "real" winery in Temecula's Southern California Wine Country. When their four children were in elementary school, the Wilson family moved to the Golden State. Gerry was heavily involved in the investment business, and Rosie became a classroom teacher.

Following retirements from their chosen professions, they heard of a small winery for sale in Riverside County. After that business opportunity failed to become a reality, they purchased a forty acre vineyard originally planted in 1969 and determined to develop their own winery. The vineyard was planted in classic varietal wine grapes: Chardonnay, Cabernet Sauvignon, Zinfandel, Pinot St. George and Roussanne.

While awaiting completion of their winery's equipment, the Wilsons produced approximately 3,000 cases of Wilson Creek wines at the Thornton Winery.

Part of the vineyard acreage that the Wilsons bought had been used as an unsightly dump site, so family and friends pitched in and hauled out more than twenty truck loads of trash - mattresses, water heaters, diesel engines and the like. Their next task was to bring in some hundred truck loads of fill dirt and begin the lengthy process of devel-

93

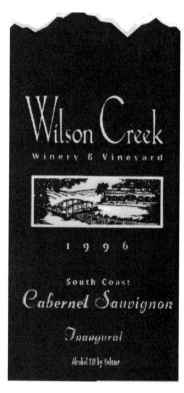

Wilson Creek Cabernet Sauvignon was the 1996 inaugural release.

oping an attractive landscape for their planned winery.

The seasonal stream at the lower boundary of the property was dubbed "Wilson Creek," and Rosie took on the assignment of planting grass, trees and flowers to enhance the ambiance. This is now a pleasant and inviting picnic area for al fresco dining or small weddings. A twenty-four-foot gazebo overlooks the wildflowers and stream and is available for special events and concerts. A nearby area is ideal for a leisurely lunch from the winery's deli along with an appropriate bottle of Wilson Creek wine.

The house on the top of the hill overlooking the vineyard is the home of Gerry and Rosie Wilson as well as their grandchildren Heather and Christopher. Son Bill and his wife Jennifer and their daughters also live on the property. Bill manages the winery, and Jennifer serves as wedding coordinator. Daughter Libby and her husband, Craig, are to run the tasting room, while son Mick, a pastor, plans to perform weddings in the gazebo or adjacent park.

Obviously, Wilson Creek is a true family project!

The address is 35960 Rancho California Road, about five miles from the I-15 freeway, and the telephone number of the winery is 693-9463.

About the Winemaker

If Gerry Wilson had known what he was facing when he envisioned building his own winery, this veteran of the investment business might have had second thoughts. The problems with developing the site and actually constructing the attractive facility that now houses Wilson Creek were indeed formidable.

One bright factor was the purchase of an existing and highly productive vineyard, now surrounded by the newest of the Temecula Valley's premium wineries. The Wilsons have become still another family to actually reside on their vineyard property and personally take part in the production and supervision of marketing of their wines.

The Wilsons are actively involved in the Temecula Valley's many wine-oriented events, and are pleased that their lengthy efforts are now a reality, so that they can now set out to accomplish their dreams for Wilson Creek.

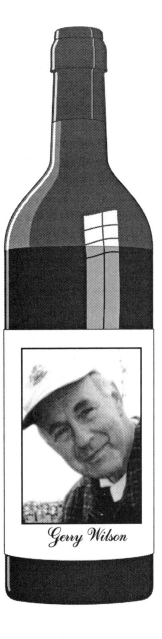

Gerry Wilson

Peacocks have appeared on Clos du Muriel labels in various colorful combinations.

Clos du Muriel

The Clos du Muriel Winery differs from other Temecula Valley wine operations in that the majority of its grapes come from other California counties.

The tasting room offers samples and is located at 33410 Rancho California Road in Temecula, approximately five miles to the east of Interstate 15.

Wines to be sampled there include Sauvignon Blanc, Fume Blanc, Merlot, Zinfandel and Sangiovese Rose from both the North Coast and the South Coast of California.

Labels bearing colorful peacocks date back to the winery's founding at another site within the Temecula Valley a number of years ago.

Temecula Valley premium estate wines include a Viognier and a Merlot, according to owner Joe Pavelich.

The tasting room offers various gift items and is open daily from 10 a.m. to 5 p.m.

There is a $4 charge for sampling seven wines and includes an attractive Clos du Muriel souvenir logo glass. For an separate one dollar, the two premium estate wines may be sampled.

Additional information may be acquired by calling 676-5400.

Wine maketh glad the heart of man.
-- Psalms 104:15

--Jon Edwards

Century old vines provide Rancho Cucamonga wineries with grapes for their own wines and other South Coast facilities as well.

Other Nearby Wineries

While this volume is essentially an account of the Temecula wine country and a description of those wineries that have made the appellation known and admired, there are a number of other wineries within close proximity that are more than worthy of a visit by wine lovers.

In the nearby Rancho Cucamonga area, for instance, the Galleano and Filippi families have maintained their historic wineries in spite of urban sprawl and the development and expansion of the Ontario International Airport.

Filippi Winery

It was 1922 when the Joseph Filippi family planted their initial vines near where the Franciscan Fathers had started their vineyards in what is recognized as "California's Oldest Wine District." At one time, the Valley was the largest grape growing district in the State. Now, fourth generation California vintners have carried on the family tradition with locations in both Rancho Cucamonga and Ontario-Guasti. With the two sites open daily for tastings, sales, gifts and special events, the family's tradition of producing a wide range of quality premium wines continues.

The Rancho Cucamonga Filippi Winery is located at 12467 Base Line Road, with tasting hours from 10 a.m. to 7 p.m. daily. The phone there is 899-5755. At the Ontario-Guasti location, 2803

East Guasti Road, hours are 9 a.m. to 6 p.m., and the number is 390-6998. Wines include old-vine Zinfandels, Cabernet Sauvignon, Sangiovese, Chardonnay, Sauvignon Blanc, and Gewurztraminer, as well as Specially-aged Ports, Sherries and Angelica.

PRODUCED & BOTTLED BY
GALLEANO WINERY
MIRA LOMA, CALIFORNIA
CONTAINS SULFITES

GALLEANO WINERY

CUCAMONGA VALLEY

Grenache Rosé

ALCOHOL 12.1% BY VOLUME   NET CONTENTS 750ML

GOVERNMENT WARNING: (1) ACCORDING TO THE SURGEON GENERAL, WOMEN SHOULD NOT DRINK ALCOHOLIC BEVERAGES DURING PREGNANCY BECAUSE OF THE RISK OF BIRTH DEFECTS. (2) CONSUMPTION OF ALCOHOLIC BEVERAGES IMPAIRS YOUR ABILITY TO DRIVE A CAR OR OPERATE MACHINERY, AND MAY CAUSE HEALTH PROBLEMS.

Galleano's 25 varietals include the classic Grenache grape.

Galleano Winery

On December 5, 1933, following the repeal of Prohibition, Domenico Galleano established the winery that still bears his name. He had purchased the land in the Wineville section of the Valley now known as Alta Loma in 1927, cultivated the sandy soil, and planted vines of European varietals. He is recognized today as an early pioneer whose vision has continued through five generations.

Today, more than 25 varietals are grown in Galleano vineyards, and the surplus not required to meet the winery's needs for its own labels is sold to other producers desiring to take advantage of the benefits of old-vine wine grapes. An unusual aspect of Galleano vines is that they are head-pruned rather than trained on the more common trellises, in the free-standing European style.

Dry farming practices lead to juices that are high in the essence of the fruit.

Don Galleano and his family now produce an array of popular wines including White Zinfandel, Cucamonga Peak White and Peak Red. An additional line of select premium wines include Zinfandel and the Rhone varietals Carignane and Grenache. Their dessert wines are award-winning choices and include proprietary "Three Friends Port," "Nino's Solera Sherry," and "Sherry Crema."

The complex at 4231 Wineville Road in Mira Loma has been designated as a Riverside County Historic landmark and as a California State Point of Historical Interest due to its working museum, of local wine history. Wine tastings from October through March are conducted from 9 a.m. to 5 p.m., Monday through Saturday and from 10:30 a.m. through 5 p.m. on Sundays. From April through September, tastings are 9 a.m. through 6 p.m. Monday through Saturday, and the Sunday hours are 10:30 a.m. through 4 p.m. Additional information may be obtained by calling 685-5376.

Rancho de Philo Winery

Rancho de Philo is named for one of the pioneer wine makers in Southern California, Philo Biane. The wine world lost the venerable Philo Biane in 1999, following a lifetime devoted to wine that lasted almost 90 years. His family continues to produce some 300 cases annually with honors from various competitions each year. A very special product of this small operation is their highly respected Triple Cream Sherry, an 18-year-old marvel that is an unbelievable bargain at $18. Here's something unusual: the winery only opens for a single week in November, and sells out the 300 cases produced within that seven day period! Call 987-4208 for details. No tours, but the winery is located at 10050 Wilson Avenue, Alta Loma.

San Diego County Wineries

Until 1893, much of what is now Southwest Riverside County was situated in San Diego County. Some 124 years earlier, Father Junipero Serra planted the initial vinifera grape cuttings at Mission San Diego and, in subsequent years, viticulturists in the area have discovered conditions conducive to the growth of premium wine grapes in such diverse locations as Escondido, Julian and Ramona. While the San Diego vineyards are not grouped as closely in proximity as those situated in the Temecula Valley to the north, they are nevertheless most interesting places to visit and enjoy the wines available for sampling and purchase there.

Deer Park Winery

Less than 20 miles south of the intersection of Rancho California Road and the I-15 Freeway in Escondido is the colorful Deer Park Winery whose labels proudly display one or more of the classic motor cars on display there. Viewing what has been described as "the world's largest auto museum of vintage convertibles" would be reason enough to visit this site, were it not for an amazing collection of Americana and the opportunity to sample fine varietal wines.

Located within 15 acres of shady oaks, orchards and vineyards, the Deer Park Winery features a gourmet deli, extensive collection of books devoted to wines and cooking, and a pleasant and

103

Vintage convertibles are featured on Deer Creek labels.

informative staff. Self-guided tours of the extensive premises and the antique car accumulation of the Knapp family of San Diego are pleasant diversions for those who stop to taste the wines of Deer Park. A vintage Helms Bakery truck awaits the visitor in the parking lot, and memorabilia of such film icons as James Dean, Marilyn Monroe and Betty Boop await inside.

Wines produced on the estate as well as those from the Napa Valley are featured, and these include Sauvignon Blanc, Johannisberg Riesling, Chardonnay, Zinfandel, Petite Sirah and Cabernet Sauvignon. The winery is just north of Lawrence Welk's Country Club at 29013 Champagne Blvd., in Escondido. For additional information, call (760) 749-1666.

Ferrara Winery

The Ferrara Winery dates back to 1919 when George Ferrara established his vineyard in what is now the bustling town of Escondido. While the original vineyard is no longer large enough to provide adequate grapes for the production of a great volume of wine, the Ferrara family is able to purchase surplus grapes from the Temecula region to the north and continue to provide their customers with quality wines. Named a State Historical Point of Interest in 1971, the winery produces and bottles several varietals including Chardonnay, Sauvignon Blanc and Nebbiolo. Estate grown Muscat of Alexandria is a specialty of the winery and a favorite of those who enjoy the fruitiness of this dessert wine. Nestled in a residential area of Escondido at 1120 W. 15th St., the Ferrara Winery is an oasis of trees and grapevines and presided over by Gaspar Ferrara and his mother, Vera. The two operate the winery and welcome guests to their modest tasting room for sampling of their distinctive and flavorful wines.

SAN DIEGO COUNTY
Muscat of Alexandria
Demi-Sec

ALCOHOL 11% BY VOLUME

PRODUCED AND BOTTLED BY
FERRARA WINERY, ESCONDIDO, CALIFORNIA

Vera and Gaspar Ferrara produce this Muscat of Alexandria dessert wine.

Orfila Winery

What is now known as Orfila Vineyards was at one time named San Pasqual, later became Jaeger and in 1993 took on its present name. It was then that Alejandro Orfila became the new owner. He is the former Argentinean Ambassador to the United States and later served consecutive terms as Secretary General of the Organization of American States. After purchasing San Diego County's largest winery and bestowing it with his family name, the Ambassador employed a knowledgeable and talented winemaker and general manager in the person of Leon Santoro. With 19 years of experience in the Napa Valley with several prestigious wineries in this region, Santoro brought to his new post extensive background in all phases of wine making and marketing.

Orfila Winery's reputation as the producer of

Orfila's Ambassador's Reserve Merlot has won many awards.

outstanding red wines has resulted from numerous awards from top wine adjudications, with the Ambassador's Reserve Merlot gaining special recognition. Other reds produced under Leon Santoro's supervision include a Sangiovese and a Syrah. Whites on the wine list include a Chardonnay, Gewurztraminer, Viognier, Johannisberg Riesling and a smooth Muscat Canelli. The winery also produces a Tawny Port, for those who enjoy a sweet after dinner red.

The winery's known locally as "The Vineyard at Escondido Golf Course," and is located at 13455 San Pasqual Road, east of the I-15 Freeway and the North County Fair shopping mall. The phone number for tours and tasting is (760) 738-6500.

Bellefleur Winery

While the Bellefleur Winery is a relative newcomer to the Southern California wine scene, its proprietors have made their mark in prior ventures. John and Martha Culbertson have owned the Fallbrook Winery since 1991 and operated the Culbertson Winery in Temecula for a number of years. The vintage Tuscan style Bellefleur opened its doors in 1997 on the perimeter of the mall known as Carlsbad Company Stores. With its own gourmet restaurant, the opportunity exists for wine lovers to wine and dine in an elegant ambiance adjacent to a mini-winery. The restaurant itself is an award-winning full-service operation with wine tasting bar and attractive gift shop. It is set among the fragrant flower fields of the area.

The address is 5610 Paseo Del Norte, just off the I-5 freeway in Carlsbad. It's open from 11 a.m. to 9 p.m. daily, and tours can be easily accommodated. Call (760) 603-1919 for details.

Wines produced by the Culbertsons under the Bellefleur label include a Pinot Noir, Chardonnay, Cabernet Sauvignon, Sauvignon Blanc and Merlot.

106

Codarossa Winery

The Codarossa Winery derives its distinctive name from the Redtail Hawks that can often be observed flying above the quaint winery located near the outskirts of the Cleveland National Forest south of the charming mountain community of Julian. Julian's annual apple crop has attracted thousands of tourists, with the community's apple pies always a delight, Many pass through the area on their way to Lake Cuyamaca and the nearby campgrounds. A visit here is worth the journey, and the winery and accompanying restaurant are open from 11 a.m. to 6 p.m. Fridays through Mondays. The mail address is P.O. Box 1926 Highway 79, Julian, California 92036. The telephone number there is (760) 765-1195.

Wines available for tasting include Petite Sirah, Merlot, Zinfandel, and Cabernet Sauvignon.

The Redtail Hawk is a symbol of the Codarossa Winery.

Menghini Winery

A few miles north of the picturesque town of Julian is the Menghini Winery, a family operation located in the midst of a lovely, old apple orchard. It's a family operation, with Mike Menghini and his wife, Toni in charge. Take either Wynola Road or Farmers Road to 1150 Julian Orchards Drive to arrive at the site, and it's a short and pleasant trip. The winery itself and tasting room accommodate a small gift shop, and is the only place that Menghini wines are offered for retail sale with the exception of several restaurants in Julian.

The tasting room is open daily from 10 a.m. to 4 p.m., and several special events are scheduled during the year taking advantage of the nearby outdoor picnic tables. This is one of the few in the region that has followed the custom of Northern California wineries by making available a bed and breakfast on the premises. The Menghini family

The Menghini Winery is noted for its Cabarnet Sauvignon. The Julian Library is featured on the winery's labels.

term theirs a "Bed and Wine" cottage, and it's located on the site and can be rented for the night. Of course, a bottle of Menghini wine is included in the price!

The winery's list includes a Cabernet Sauvignon, Chardonnay, Muscat Canelli, White Riesling, and Sauvignon Blanc as well as several blends and (of course) a prize winning apple wine. For details of events held at the winery, call (760) 765-2072.

Witch Creek Winery

The distinctive Witch Creek labels designate wines made from grapes purchased from various sources in both San Diego and Riverside Counties. Kathy and Dave Wodehouse operate a pair of tasting rooms to showcase (and retail) their wines,

including a Zinfandel, Mourvedre, Sauvignon Blanc, Cabernet, Grenache, Merlot, Syrah, Nebbiolo, Carignane and several fruit wines.

Look for their outlets in the heart of the quaint town of Julian at 2000 Main Street and in downtown Carlsbad, at 2906 Carlsbad Blvd. in Carlsbad Village between I-5 and the Pacific Coast Highway. The Carlsbad location not only offers a tasting room, but also has available many gift items, gourmet foods and an art gallery featuring local artists. The winery's "Muscat Love," is a white dessert wine made from the Muscat Canelli grape with a name reminiscent of the popular Captain and Tennille recording.

Call (760) 720-7499 for additional details.

Witch Creek's creative labels reflect the owner's sense of humor.

Shadow Mountain Winery

Sunshine Summit is located on the old Butterfield Stage Route on what is now Highway 79 north of Warner Springs. The vineyards in the area date back to just after World War II and have served to provide more than one Southern California winery with grapes over the years. The 3500 feet elevation provides the warmth of summer sun along with the coolness of Pacific Ocean breezes for ideal grape growing conditions, making this a unique microclimate similar to that of the Temecula Valley several miles to the north.

The Shadow Mountain label belongs to the McGeary family, Pam and Alex, and their 18 acres produce the majority of grapes used in their wines, Viognier, Zinfandel, Muscat, Carignane, Mourvedre, Grenache and Chardonnay. The winery is a family operation, and don't be surprised to find Alex busily applying labels to one of his premium varietal wines. The present winery was rebuilt in 1997, following a devastating forest fire that took place two years earlier.

Sampling is available at their 35124 Highway 79 location Tuesdays through Sunday from 10 a.m.

Shadow Mountain

VINEYARDS

1997

SOUTH COAST
SYRAH

PRODUCED AND BOTTLED BY
SHADOW MOUNTAIN VINEYARDS
WARNER SPRINGS, CALIFORNIA
ALCOHOL 11.6% BY VOLUME NET CONTENTS 750 ML

*The label depicts the
sunshine summit
overlooking Shadow
Mountain Winery.*

through 5 p.m., and Pam presides over a well-attended Champagne Sunday Brunch from 10 a.m. to 2 p.m. One may phone (760) 782-0778 for additional directions to this winery, a pleasant drive south of the Temecula Wine Country.

Bernardo Winery

San Diego's Bernardo Winery is one of the oldest continuously operating wineries in the State, dating back to 1889 and a Spanish Land Grant. It's presided over by genial Ross Rizzo and his sons. The Rizzo family has been making wines for five generations after coming to America from Palermo, Sicily, and settling in Southern California. With some 75 acres of vineyards and olive trees, the setting is a charming trip to yesterday surrounded by the upscale community of Rancho Bernardo.

Unique among other wineries in San Diego County, Bernardo Winery also produces cold-pressed, virgin olive oil and wine vinegar, only available at the colorful tasting room. Wine sampling includes Merlot, Zinfandel, Cabernet Sauvignon, Chianti, Sangiovese, Syrah, Mourvedre, Barbera and Grenache. Whites available for tasting include Chablis, White Riesling, Chardonnay, Gewurztraminer and Muscat Canelli.

Grape sources are from San Diego County , South Coast, Temecula and Rancho Cucamonga vineyards. In addition to the above, Bernardo Winery's tasting room offers three dessert wines, Muscatel, Cream Sherry and Port, as well as a large assortment of fruit wines and honey mead. The Rizzo family initially purchased the winery in 1928 and managed to outlive the Prohibition years by selling sacramental wine and fresh grape juice. The juice, incidentally, was guaranteed to begin the fermentation process as soon as the buyers arrived at their homes.

The grounds of the winery contain a large park and picnic area with adjacent Winery Village Shops, where a variety of personable shop

Bernardo Winery is San Diego's oldest operating vineyard and winery.

111

owners offer unusual and attractive gifts and services. On Fridays, a Farmers Market is held on the grounds, attracting visitors from all over the area to shop for farm-fresh produce, flowers and specialties.

Bernardo Winery is located to the east of I-15 at Pomerado Road to 13330 Paseo Del Verano Norte. The telephone number for information is (619) 487-1866,and the hours of operation are 9 a.m. to 5 p.m. daily including Sundays.

Schwaesdall Winery

"Ramona" may be best known for being the name of the heroine of Helen Hunt Jackson's story of life in early California. But the town of Ramona in San Diego County may at some point be as well known as the home of John Schwaesdall's winery. With five acres currently under production, the roofing contractor has found the time to make a name for himself in the commercial wine world. The latest addition to his winery is a tasting room constructed of plastered bales of straw, insulated to maintain a year-round temperature conducive to ideal wine storage, while fulfilling the dual need of an attractive tasting room. It's not likely that the Big Bad Wolf will ever be able to huff and puff and blow this straw house down!

John's wines are stored and aged under his adobe house in a cellar that once served as the winery's tasting room. The loamy soil of the vineyard and other South Coast sources produce a number of varietal wines including Cabernet Sauvignon, Chardonnay, Merlot, Mourvedre, Zinfandel, Carignane, Syrah, Petite Sirah and Sauvignon Blanc. A house specialty is a delightful "Cuvee de Oro." Wines are aged in both French and American oak, and the tasting room is open weekends from 10 a.m. to 6 p.m. Visitors will enjoy the various rock formations dotting the vineyard as well as the impressive view of neighboring

Go thy way, eat thy bread with joy, and drink thy wine with a merry heart.

--Ecclesiastes 9:7

112

Iron Mountain.

The Schwaesdall Winery is located between Poway and the town of Ramona off State Highway 67 at 177677 Rancho de Oro Road. Call (760) 789-7547 for additional directions and news of special events.

Other vineyards in San Diego County provide grapes for operating wineries and may go into production in future years as independent labels. Still more vineyard owners are content to grow their premium varietal grapes and sell them to others in the South Coast area.

1997
Estate Bottled
Merlot
South Coast

Produced and Bottled by Schwaesdall Winery
Ramona, California
Alcohol 12.5% by volume

John Schwaesdall is known for his estate-bottled Merlot.

113

Baja California Wineries

Many wine lovers' first experience with the wines of Baja California came while on a vacation to Mazatlan or Ensenada. They had heard that the Franciscan Friars had planted Mission grapes as they accompanied the Spanish conquistadors into the New World. The first varietal grapevines arrived in Baja California with the founding of the Mission of Saint Tomas Aquinas in 1791. The wines of Baja that were first sold in Alta California were those produced by the Santo Tomas Winery of Ensenada.

In 1857, the Mexican federal government decreed the nationalization of all church holdings, and the fertile Santo Tomas Valley then became property of the State. Don Loreto Amador later acquired the vineyards located on that acreage and began making wine on a commercial basis. In 1888, new owners bought the property and founded what is known as Bodegas de Santo Tomas, now headquartered in downtown Ensenada.

Santo Tomas

With more than a century of wine making experience, Santo Tomas takes full advantage of the opportunity they have of producing quality wines from the cultivation of noble grapes grown in optimal climactic conditions in appropriate soils. A popular Santo Tomas wine is their Barbera, a dry and full-bodied red with the bouquet of hazelnuts and spices. In addition, Santo Tomas produces a Bordeaux-style blend known as Duetto and a delightful wine made from the Tempranillo grape, a varietal from the Rioja Valley in northern Spain.

Santo Tomas is located at Avenida Miramar No. 666, Zona Centro, Ensenada, Baja California, Mexico, and the telephone number from the United States is (011 52) (61) 78 33 33.

Casa Pedro Domecq

In the Guadalupe Valley, some 20 miles north of Ensenada is the Domecq Winery, recipient of many awards in international competitions. It was in 1791 that the Franciscan Friars discovered the soils of the Guadalupe Valley and planted vineyards in what is now known as Bodega de las Misiones. The Mediterranean climate here is similar to that of Temecula, in that the warm days are cooled in the evening by fresh breezes from Pacific Ocean on the west.

Casa Pedro Domecq offers a wide spectrum of premium wines including the following reds: Cabernet Sauvignon, Zinfandel, Merlot and a number of others unique to the winery. Their whites include Sauvignon Blanc, Chardonnay, a White Zinfandel and other proprietary blends.

With 3,000 acres of vineyards surrounding the casa, the winery offers guided tours, tasting and sales Monday though Friday from 10 a.m. to 4 p,m, and Saturdays from 10 a.m. to 1:30 p.m. The phone number in Mexico is 01615-52249.

L.A. Cetto Winery

Closer to the United States border in Tijuana is the celebrated L.A. Cetto Winery, located at Cañon Johnson No. 2108, Esquina Av. Constitucion Sur, Col. Hidalgo. When Don Angelo Cetto arrived in Baja California in 1926, he brought with him the solid tradition in viticulture that resulted in the award-winning winery that today

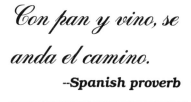

Con pan y vino, se anda el camino.

--**Spanish proverb**

bears his family name. More than 70 years after its beginnings, the third generation of the Cetto family continues to grow its grapes in the fertile Valle de Guadalupe.In 1983, the first bottles with the L.A. Cetto label appeared on the market, and began to win awards for the quality of its wines. Reds in the Cetto line include Nebbiolo, Cabernet Sauvignon, Petite Sirah and Zinfandel, while the premium whites are a Chardonnay, Fumé Blanc, Chenin Blanc, Riesling and two blush wines, a Blanc de Colombard and a Blanc de Zinfandel.

The tasting rooms permit guests to observe the aging process of this proud Baja California winery as well as taste the wines of L.A. Cetto as they walk through the cellar. A boutique offers a wide assortment of items related to the art of wine making. Tour hours are Monday through Saturday from 10 a.m. to 5:30 p.m. and the tour is free with tasting at $1 with a souvenir wine glass one dollar more.The phone number in Mexico is (66) 85 30 31 for additional information.

Chateau Camou Winery

Chateau Camou is another Baja California that is gaining recognition in the States for its products. Also nestled in the heart of the verdant Guadalupe Valley is Mexico's youngest winery. For a winery tour and additional information, the Mexican phone number in Ensenada is (011) 52 (61) 77 22 21.

Monte Xanic Winery

Monte Xanic is still another winery located in the Valle de Guadalupe and often one visited by wine lovers touring Baja's wine country. Winery tours are by appointment only, but the retail store is located behind the Plaza Civica at Baja Naval Boatyard in Ensenada. The phone number there is (011) 52 (61) 78 31 46.

Sean Murphy and Nancy Shockley enjoy lunch and a spectacular view of the Callaway Vineyard as they dine at the Vineyard Terrace Cafe.

Dining
in the Wine Country

Those visiting the Temecula Valley's premium wineries do not lack for opportunities to dine, as both gourmet restaurants and numerous fast-food outlets are to be found in the area. Visitors planning to stay overnight will be pleased to know that lodging is also available. All telephone numbers in the following listings are in the 909 area code; in February, 2000, the area code will change to 951.

Café Champagne

The first restaurant to be located at a winery is the celebrated Café Champagne at Thornton Winery, presided over by Executive Chef Steve Pickell. The restaurant features California-style cuisine with a menu created to complement the varietal wines produced at Thornton. An herb garden greets visitors entering from the parking area, and this supplies the fresh seasonings used in preparing items on the well-balanced menu. Café Champagne is a multi-year winner of the prestigious Gold Award from the Southern California Restaurant Writers. Specials change daily, and bread is baked each morning. Special occasions and corporate events can be scheduled by contacting 699-0099. The Thornton Winery is located at 32575 Rancho California Road, four miles from the Interstate 15 junction. It is part of the impressive Thornton complex, and the first winery encountered on the right side of the highway. Open

119

daily from 11 a.m. to 9 p.m., except on Mondays when hours are 11 a.m. to 4 p.m., this is an ideal site for that special dining treat.

Baily Wine Country Café

Baily Wine Country Café continues to provide visitors and local residents alike with top quality California/Continental cuisine at a moderate price. The relaxed and cozy atmosphere is matched with friendly and knowledgeable service. Menu items are prepared fresh and include truly "work of art" dessert options. Operated by Chris Baily of the family that oversees the Baily and Temecula Crest Wineries, the Café features many of the fine Temecula Valley varietal wines by the glass or bottle. A special feature of this restaurant is the popular "Picnics to Go" choice. Those who plan Wine Country tasting trips or country excursions may call the Café with at least twenty-four hours advance notice, and a gourmet picnic basket will await their arrival.

The Baily Wine Country Café is located in the Rancho California Town Center, 27644 Ynez Road, just to the east of Interstate 15. For information, call 676-9567. Reservations are recommended, and both lunch and dinner are served in either the restaurant itself or in the colorful sidewalk patio.

Vineyard Terrace Cafe

A couple of years ago, master chef Steve Fohl and his wife, Diane, convinced the folks at Callaway Vineyard & Winery that he should open an intimate restaurant on the balcony above the impressive vista of Callaway grape vines. It was an immediate success, and now the Vineyard Terrace offers a menu featuring Mediterranean cuisine that complements the outstanding Callaway wines produced nearby. The menu isn't at all static, as it depends on the freshest ingredients available and the creative chef's imagination. It's right on the premises of Temecula largest winery, 32720 Rancho California Road. Open for lunch from Thursday to Sunday and Friday and Saturday for dinner, it's a good idea to call ahead as seating is somewhat limited, and special Callaway events may be scheduled. The number is 308-6661, and the dining experience is bound to be a memorable one.

The Exchange on Washington

Kirk Dye's popular "Come Sea" restaurant is ten minutes north of Temecula in quiet Murrieta, to the west of Interstate 15 at 24910 Washington Avenue. From the crusty sourdough bread served at the beginning of each repast to the tasty desserts, a true dining experience awaits guests.

Mesquite-grilled "fresh and only fresh" seafoods, steaks, pastas, grilled artichokes, steamed clams and smoked albacore are featured on the extensive menu. It's not unusual to be seated beside one or more of the Temecula Valley's distinguished winemakers at the The Exchange, where local wines are always available to complement the meals, For directions or reservations, call 677-9449.

Temecula Pizza Company

This is not an ordinary pizza restaurant but one offering fine dining with pizzas featuring a special white sauce, fresh pears, gorgonzola cheese and pine nuts as well as sun-dried tomato salad with homemade dressing.

The restaurant is attractively decorated, and there is ample room for patio dining. Each of the items is freshly made on the premises. The Temecula Pizza Company is located south of Rancho California Road at 44535 Bedford Court, on Highway 79 off Interstate 15. The phone number is 694-9463.

Stuart Anderson's Black Angus

The Temecula version of this popular chain of restaurants is nearly always packed with guests who appreciate the ambience and menu offerings. Located at 27735 Ynez Road, across from the Rancho California Town Center, and just north of the intersection of Interstate 15 and Rancho California Road, this is the place folks go when they want a steak and all the trimmings cooked just right. Reservations are suggested, and the number to call is 699-8000.

The Claim Jumper

If one is interested in large portions of tasty food, then the Claim Jumper is the place to dine; almost everyone is observed carrying out a doggie bag! A menu that covers just about all the possible menu items to please any palate awaits guests, and ample parking is available. No reservations are needed, since guests are seated upon arrival. The Temecula Claim Jumper Restaurant is also located in the Rancho California Town Center at 29370 Rancho California Road. The telephone number is 694-6887.

Colombo's Vineyard Restaurant

Located at 29000 Front Street in Old Temecula near Interstate 15 and the Highway 79 intersection, this friendly restaurant attracts those who appreciate homestyle cooking in an environment of bright colors and attentive servers. It's open for breakfast, lunch and dinner, and reservations aren't necessary. For details or additional information, call 695-5390.

Penfold's Café

An institution in the Temecula Valley and located to the southwest of the Intersection of Interstate 15 and Rancho California Road in Old Town, Penfold's has a varied menu and a staff that aims to meet diners' needs. The steady stream of customers attests to the fact that Penfold's is successful in its mission. Open at 5:30 a.m., the restaurant serves breakfast, lunch and dinner at 28250 Front Street. Call 676-6411 for details.

Trattoria Bacio

This traditional full-service Italian restaurant opened in 1999 at 27315 Jefferson Avenue in Temecula, featuring a lunch and dinner menu with a wide range of pastas, seafood, milk-fed veal and chicken entrees. The antipastos, salads and soups all have that Italian style, and the service is always prompt and pleasant. Call 699-4428 for additional information. Owner Robert Gallo's extensive wine list contains numerous varietals from Temecula vineyards.

Mille Luce

Another new and well-reviewed restaurant featuring a continental cuisine with the emphasis on Mediterranean fare is Mille Luce. It's located at 32475 Clinton Keith Road in Wildomar, to the west of I-15, and is noted for its osso buco in Marsala wine sauce. The home made desserts are another feature of this attractive setting. On Thursday through Saturday, there is usually a piano bar in operation to provide a musical ambiance for dining and dancing. Call 609-1266 for details.

Oscar's

San Diego-based Oscar's opened its Temecula

branch in 1998 to an enthusiastic and appreciative group of customers. The chain has as its Mission Statement: "To make great tasting, home made food from the freshest, highest quality ingredients and to serve it quickly in a clean, friendly and relaxed atmosphere." The crowds lining up daily at Oscar's are proof enough of the success of this venture. In Temecula, Oscar's is 23975 Rancho California Road, near the intersection of I-15 and adjacent to the Temecula Duck Pond. It's dedicated to families, and the hearty portions and ample menu appeal to all ages. No need for reservations, and be sure to check out Oscar's famous bread sticks.

The Mill

While creative pizza and pastas are featured on the menu, The Mill isn't really another Italian restaurant. It's another Kirk Dye eatery and a worthy companion to his popular Exchange a few blocks away. This one is at 24690 Washington Avenue in Murrieta, and features an impressive cellar of Temecula wines and microbrewed beers to accompany his specialty menu items. Those leaving The Mill have been overheard expressing admiration for the sun-dried tomato salad dressing as well as the tasty pizza crusts and the obvious warmth of the caring serving staff. For directions or reservations, please call 677-0960.

Fujiyama

Located at 30680 Rancho California Road, about half-way between the Temecula Wine Country and I-15, this Japanese restaurant is a favorite of many who favor Oriental cuisine. With a popular sushi bar and a bank of teppan-yaki grills, the menu offers both luncheon specials and a wide range of combination dinners. The service is always welcome, and young diners seem to enjoy the theatrics of the animated chefs. It's in the shop-

Diogenes was asked what wine he liked best; and he answered as I would have done when he said: "Somebody else's."
—**Michel de Montaigne**

124

ping center near Long's Drug Store at Margarita Road, and the phone number is 676-6484.

Sicilian Cowboy

When you're looking for genuine Italian specialties such as bisteccia griglia and pollo oreganiti, this is the place to go! The Sicilian Cowboy's ambiance is that of a Clint Eastwood "spaghetti western film," and the menu is an authentic one with sauces and seafood typical of the Isle of Sicily. Located in Murrieta at 40942 California Oaks Road, the restaurant is open for both lunch and dinner. Call 676-6484 for additional details

Mimi's Cafe

The Temecula site of this Southern California chain of restaurants is located at 40825 Winchester Road. east of the I-15 interchange. If one has dined at another Mimi's location, then the French farmhouse ambiance here will be a familiar one. The luncheon and dinner bill of fare features such varied entrees as Cajun and New Orleans specialties. One of the few major Temecula restaurants open for breakfast, Mimi's offers an outstanding variety of appetite pleasers. The phone there is 694-0664.

Chappy's Roadhouse

If sawdust and peanut shells on the floor aren't a problem, then this is the place for you! Barbecued beef sandwiches, succulent pork ribs, coleslaw and beans are menu favorites, and the jukebox can be counted on to be playing oldies as well as country hits. Free peanuts are offered at the door along with a cup to fill, as the friendly staff points to a printed menu on the wall to determine diner's pleasure. Open for lunch and dinner, Chappy's in located in the middle of the Target Center at 27476 Ynez Road in Temecula. It's the kind of roadhouse that is part of America's automotive and dining history, transplanted to the midst of a outdoor shopping mall. No reservations required, and entertainment is a frequent weekend diversion. Call 587-0055 for details.

Tony's Spunky Steer

The Temecula location of this informal Southern California restaurant is located at 27645 Jefferson Avenue, on the west side of the I-15 freeway. The menu features all sorts of mouth-watering old-fashioned treats including chicken-fried steaks, chicken dishes, liver and onions, and home-made pies. A coat and tie aren't required for service, just a good appetite and pleasant smile to match that of the servers. Tony's is designed for a family trade, and the bright and airy atmosphere is ideal for casual dining Monday through Sunday, 11 a.m., to 9 p.m. The telephone number in Temecula is 676-1963.

The Temet Grill

Located on the grounds of the Temecula Creek Inn, the Temet Grill has gained fame as one of the area's gourmet restaurants. Under the supervision of talented chef Brian Johnson, the Temet Grill continues to provide award-winning meals at one of the Temecula Valley's most elegant sites. While the menu is subject to seasonal variations, one can always count on attractively prepared and presented dining treats. The lush green golf course environment is conducive to good conversation as well as epicurean dining, and the wine list features many local varietal favorites. Open for breakfast, lunch and dinner, the children's menu is a comprehensive one. It's located at 44501 Rainbow Canyon Road south of the Wine Country, and the phone at the Temet Grill is 694-1000.

Prestos Gourmet Express

Daily specials and the scent of fresh baked

breads are what Prestos customers have come to expect at this informal restaurant located at 30590 Rancho California Road, near the intersection with Margarita Road to the west of the Temecula Wine Country in the Lucky Center's Palomar Village. With modest prices and super service, it's often the lunch and dinner destination of Wine Country staff members. Owner Ron Paine even has his own private label Nebbiolo wine produced and bottled by the nearby Mount Palomar Winery. Daily specials vary the bill of fare, and it's never too difficult to catch a server's eye. Their telephone number is 699-0019.

Marie Callender Restaurant

Anyone who has ever eaten at a Marie Callender's knows what to expect: a full menu of favorite items, cooked just right and served with a smile along with great baked goods. Don't forget to take home a pie for later dining pleasure. Located at 29363 Rancho California Road, at the intersection of Ynez and the Temecula Duck Pond, this newer Temecula Restaurant has fast become a favorite of local residents as well as visitors.

The telephone is 699-9339, and Marie Callender's is adjacent to the expanded Embassy Suites Hotel.

Scarcella's Italian Grill & Spirits

A long-time favorite of local diners at its prior location, the new Scarcella's has attracted a crowd of brand new fans to its enchanting and friendly location in the center of the Tower Plaza Shopping Center at 27525 Ynez Road, in Temecula. It's probably the only place in California that one can order pizza marguerita, although more well-known menu items such as eggplant parmesan and a full scope of pasta dishes remain. Reservations may be made by calling 676-5450, and both lunch and dinner are served. With over 120 seating capacity,

Joe and Pat Scarcella's is a frequent destination for parties and family celebrations.

Nihon Japanese Restaurant

Located in the Target Center at 27576 Ynez Road is the praised Nihon Japanese Restaurant. The excellent sushi bar continues to be a magnet for those who prefer this exotic dish in addition to the traditional sukiyaki, teriyaki, sashimi and tempura entrees or the popular combinations with pork, chicken or steak. Lunch and dinner are served, and the phone number at Nihon is 699-8589.

If I ever met a girl with kisses like wine, I'd marry her on the spot.

--W.C. Fields

Pechanga Cafe

The only local restaurant to be located on an Indian Reservation and open 24 hours is the Cafe at the Pechanga Entertainment Center to the west of the Temecula Wine Country. Somewhat similar to Las Vegas operations of the same nature, this site offers no bar or wine list, but the bountiful servings leave little room for extras. The buffet is one of the most extensive in the area and a full menu is available for those who prefer more formal dining experiences. The all-you-can-eat Sunday Brunch attracts a large and appreciative crowd. There's an ambiance of fun and occasional musical groups that accompany repasts, and plenty of opportunities to test one's skill at various games in the surrounding casino. The Pechanga Entertainment Center is located at 45000 Pala Road in Temecula, and the phone is 693-1819.

Fish House Vera Cruz

Another San Diego-based chain has discovered that Temecula is a promising site to open a new restaurant, and the Fish House Vera Cruz is an excellent example of how such an expansion can prove to be a wise business move. The crowds of those who appreciate the delicacies of properly grilled fish demonstrate that there's always room for another gourmet experience. The appetizers as well as the soups prepare diners for a balanced selection of seafood entrees. No need to call, as reservations aren't accepted. The address is 26700 Ynez Road, in Temecula, just south of the auto mall. The phone there is 506-2899.

Sizzler Restaurant

The flagship location of Gary and Sally Myers' fleet of Sizzler Restaurants is located at 27717 Jefferson Avenue in Temecula. It has all the features of the well-known chain of Sizzlers, and some special additions, too. It's the popular site of numerous local clubs for their regular meetings, where members take advantage of both the full menu of steaks and seafood along with an amazing salad bar with a great assortment of do-it-yourself items. The Sunday Brunch always attracts a large crowd of appreciative diners.

Hours occasionally change, so call 676-3630 for current times. Lunch and dinner patrons can expect both tasty food and excellent service.

Rockin' Baja Lobster

One might think he or she was actually south of the border in Baja California upon entering the Rockin' Baja Lobster restaurant at 27511 Ynez Road in Temecula. The environment and menu both reflect management's attempt to recreate the style and ambiance of one of the finer Baja California eateries.

While seafood (as the name implies) is the house specialty, there are others on the menu from north of the border. With a full bar featuring Mexican beers, it's open daily for both lunch and dinner. The phone at Rockin' Baja Lobster is 694-8119.

Hungry Hunter

This restaurant claims to serve the "best prime rib in town," and there are a number of loyal fans of the Hungry Hunter who would agree. With prime rib and signature choice steaks, few leave the premises still craving food. Serving copious portions of well-prepared entrees on every plate, luncheon is served Monday through Friday and dinners are a nightly feature. Banquet rooms are available, and reservations are gladly accepted. It's located at 27600 Jefferson Avenue in Temecula, and the phone number is 694-1475.

Rocky Cola Cafe

An old-fashioned cafe with a juke box and home style cooking is to be found at the Rocky Cola Cafe in Temecula. It's located at 27405 Jefferson Avenue, between Rancho California Road and Winchester. There's a special menu for those who are on various health-related diets, and the portions are more than ample.

Rarely a need for reservations, but the number there is 699-9667.

Pirates of the Caribbean

Dining "Pirate Style" on the table means messy fun here, but the innovative cuisine at this restaurant located in Temecula's "Old Town" at 41925 Third Street always provides an unusual dining experience. The menu includes crab, lobster, clams, mussels and shrimp as well as chicken and steak. The buckets of beer come in handy for parties and a rollicking evening. Eye patches and peg legs aren't required. For details, call 695-1405.

The Captain's Cabin

Fresh seafood would be expected at any restaurant called "The Captain's Cabin." but this admired Temecula dining institution also offers a wide range of steaks, prime rib and evening specials. Open for dinner only from Tuesday through Sunday from 5 p.m., The Captain's Table is located to the west of the I-15 freeway at 28551 Rancho California Road. With a full-service bar and private banquet rooms, this is another festive site for company parties and family gatherings in a nautical setting. Closed Mondays with entertainment and dancing on weekends, the number for reservations is 676-9334.

Temeku Hills Grill Room

The Grill Room at the Temeku Hills Country Club has become a landmark for special events in a brief time since its recent opening in 1998. There's a panoramic view of the surrounding mountains as well as the adjacent golf course. With a glass enclosed restaurant, the Grill Room is open for breakfast, lunch and dinner and a popular Sunday Brunch. The banquet facilities can accommodate groups from 50 to one thousand diners. The address is 41687 Temeku Drive, just to the east of Margarita and Rancho California Road. The phone there is 694-9998, and there are ample opportunities for either indoor or patio dining.

Richie's Real American Diner

Nostalgia buffs will want to stop by Richie's Real American Diner for what amounts to an All-American home-cooked meal. The meat loaf is just like Mother always tried to make, and the baked goods are fresh and mouth-watering. It's a trip back to the time when diners were everywhere in America, and among the best places to get a full meal at a fair price.

Located to the north of Winchester Road at 27313 Jefferson Avenue in Temecula, Richie's is a great place to take the family for a dining-out experience. The phone there is 695-2500.

131

Loma Vista guests enjoy a panoramic view of the Temecula Valley.

Lodging in the Wine Country

Loma Vista Bed & Breakfast

For those who wish to enjoy a stay in an award-winning Bed & Breakfast located in the heart of the Temecula Wine Country, the lovely mission-style Loma Vista is ideal. Nestled among premium vineyards and citrus groves, Loma Vista's guest rooms offer peace and quiet and the serenity of an unparalleled view of the surrounding mountains. Innkeepers Walt and Sheila Kurezynski have made the comfort of their guests their first consideration, and the proof of their success lies in the many repeat visits of previous guests.

All rates are based on double occupancy and include wine and cheese in the evening and a full champagne breakfast in the morning. Six exceptional guest rooms and a caring staff make any visit a refreshing and memorable experience. For detailed information or reservations in this non-smoking inn, call 676-7047. Loma Vista is located approximately five miles east of Interstate 15 off Rancho California Road within walking distance of several wineries.

Temecula Creek Inn

This resort features all the amenities one could wish for and is located just a few miles south of the Wine Country in the rolling hills of Southern

133

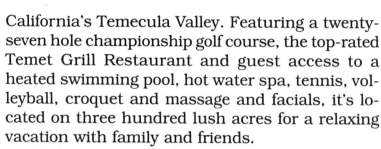

California's Temecula Valley. Featuring a twenty-seven hole championship golf course, the top-rated Temet Grill Restaurant and guest access to a heated swimming pool, hot water spa, tennis, volleyball, croquet and massage and facials, it's located on three hundred lush acres for a relaxing vacation with family and friends.

Eighty rooms overlook the valley and arrangements can be made for Wine Country bike tours, the sixteen-mile mountain bike ride down scenic Palomar Mountain, hot air ballooning and tickets to nearby special musical events.

Packages including accommodations, meals and activities may be reserved by calling 676-5631. Temecula Creek Inn is located off Indio/Highway 79 exit of Interstate 15 at 44501 Rainbow Canyon Road in Temecula.

Embassy Suites

Located at the major intersection of Interstate 15 and Rancho California Road, across from the community's Duck Pond, Temecula's Embassy Suites boast 176 two-room elegantly appointed luxury suites. Complimentary made-to-order breakfasts and evening beverages are included in guests' stay, and full banquet and meeting room facilities are available.

Nearby attractions, in addition to the Temecula Wine Country, include many restaurants, the shops and antique stores of Old Town Temecula, championship golf courses and hot air balloon rides. A fitness center, outdoor Olympic-size pool and whirlpool are among the amenities available to guests. The Embassy Suites local number is 676-5656 and a direct toll-free number from other locations is (800) 416-6116.

Best Western Country Inn

Featuring seventy-four spacious rooms professionally decorated with elegant touches and fine quality furniture, the Country Inn is just a few miles from the Wine Country. A continental breakfast, heated pool, spa and sauna await the Inn's guests, and special luxurious suites with in-room spas, wet bars, refrigerators and fireplaces are available.

Old Town Temecula is less than a mile away and the Wine Country is located within six miles. Special weekday rates are featured along with free HBO and satellite channels.

The Country Inn is located at 27706 Jefferson Avenue, Temecula, and the toll-free number for reservations is (800) 528-1234, while a direct line to the Inn is 676-7378. Ask about the golf, spa and romance packages.

Comfort Inn

With seventy-two bright and comfortable rooms, the Comfort Inn is located near Old Town, the Temecula Wine Country, golf courses and is within walking distance to fine restaurants. A pool, hot tub and complimentary coffee and sweet rolls await guests each morning.

It's located at 27338 Jefferson Avenue, in Temecula. The number for reservations is either 699-5888 or (800) 228-5150

Butterfield Inn

The quaint 39-room Butterfield Inn takes guests back to the days of the Butterfield Stage route through the heart of Old Town Temecula. It reflects the charm and atmosphere of the 1880s and is located in the midst of the numerous gift and antique shops of the area.

Located at 28718 Front Street, its phone number is 676-4833.

Palomar Hotel

Old Town Temecula is the site of the community's efforts to relive the sights and sounds of yesterday and the Palomar Hotel is located near the center of the colorful restaurants and stores that make up Front Street. With only 10 rooms, the Palomar Hotel is usually booked solid during weekends, but a call to 676-6503 may reveal available space. It's a good idea to call well in advance of potential visits, and the ambiance and closeness to Old Town make this a memorable lodging experience. The address is 28522 Front Street

Temecula Valley Inn

Great accommodations await guests at Temecula's newest hotel, the Temecula Valley Inn. It's centrally located at 27660 Jefferson Avenue, to the west off the I-15 freeway and just north of Rancho California Road. It features 90 deluxe and business class guest rooms, non-smoking suites, and a conference room. With free continental breakfasts, cable, refrigerators, pool and spa, this is rapidly becoming a popular destination. Both shopping and restaurants are within walking distance, and the Wine Country and a dozen or so of California's premium wineries are a few minutes away from the Inn. Call 699-2444 for rates and details of the special "Getaway Weekend for Two" including limousine, breakfast, dinner champagne and a hot air balloon ride.

Rancho California RV Resort

For those visiting the Temecula Wine Country in their recreational vehicles, this is the spot for you! Located on Highway 79 South, just 18 miles from Temecula, it's a place to rest by the lake or hike in the mountains. All sorts of amenities are available to guests, as well as the opportunity to just chill out and have a relaxing time.

The completed resort is planned for 810 sites, an 18 hole golf course, a 20,000 sq. ft. clubhouse and five swimming pools. For additional information and a map, please write Post Office Box 67. 45525 Highway 79 South, Aguana, California 92536. The toll-free phone number is (888) 767-0848.

Pala Mesa Resort

Located in the peaceful foothills of North San Diego's wine country, the Pala Mesa Resort features 133 large and comfortable rooms. Adjacent to a championship par 72 golf course, there are additional lighted tennis courts, a fitness center and spa and full service restaurant with lounge. Meeting and banquet space is available with attractive outdoor terraces. Special golf packages are available year round. It's located at 2001 Old Hwy. 395 in Fallbrook. The telephone number is (760) 728-5881.

About the Author

Vick Knight, Jr., Ed.D., is an award-winning amateur winemaker. A former regional director of *Les Amis du Vin*, he conducts occasional classes in wine appreciation for both consumers and professionals. He assists restaurateurs in the development of menus to complement their cuisines and writes a wine column for *The Press-Enterprise*.

Dr. Knight is a retired educator and the author of more than twenty books and numerous articles on a wide range of topics. He is a graduate of the University of Southern California and an unabashed fan of the various wines produced from varietal grapes of the Muscat family.

He lives fifteen miles north of the Temecula Wine Country, in Canyon Lake, California, with his wife, Carolyn, an author, editor and consumer health advocate.

139

Order Form

Additional copies of "Toasting Temecula Wines" may be ordered by using this form.

Please send me _____ copies of the revised edition of "Toasting Temecula Wines"
    @ $12.95 each.   _____

California residents add 97¢ tax per book.   _____

Handling and mailing, $3 for first book,
    and $1 for each additional copy.   _____

TOTAL   _____

MAIL ORDERS TO:

Name _____

Address_____

City, State, Zip _____

Send check or mail order, made payable to
Aristan Press
22597 Canyon Lake Dr. South
Canyon Lake, CA 92587-7595